style

Quacks Books

Q

dedication

Access and **excellence** are within the power of the *artisan*; **care** and attempting to be **effective** are his *benchmark*.

The **knowledge** that, by *trying* each day, he will **progress** and constantly feel *uplifted* in the beauty of his **craft**, is his *reward*.

Where we mention he in this book, we include men and women.

To style or not to style?
That is the question.

A Story of the Book.

Michael Sessions

Quacks Books,
7 Grape Lane, Petergate
and 53 Petergate, York

printed by Quacks the Printers

iv

Published by **Quacks Books**
7 Grape Lane, Petergate, York.

British Library cataloguing in publication data
The **John Jackson** Trust 1992
A Story of the Book, entitled *To style*, or not to style?
That is the question.
Great Britain.

ISBN: 978-1-912728-63-3
E-Book ISBN: 978-1-912728-65-7

First edition 1992,
Second edition 2010, extensively revised and enlarged,
published for the *quincentenary* of the birth of *book printing*
in the North of England at York, 18ᵗʰ February 2010.

Third edition 2023, revised and enlarged to include
55 years of the Sessions Book Trust and 5 years of a
younger generation at Jackson House.

edited by **Michael H Sessions**
Martin Nelson, Rachel Hopkins.

Obtainable directly by post from the publisher or your local bookshops or even Amazon.

Set in the *typeface* **Baskerville** twelve-point roman with occasional text **emboldening** and *italicising*, with one and half point inter line leading, headings *ranged left* in *eighteen point* **Baskerville bold**, page size 215mm x 215 mm with an inside margin, *gutter* of 15 mm, top margin, *head* of 25mm and outside margin or *for-edge* of 30mm.
The bottom margin, *foot* is 35mm.

Illustrated with *lithographs*, *etchings*, *engravings* and *wood cuts*
and one or two specially commissioned *prints* and *paintings*.

Printed by *offset lithography* on 100gsm **book wove**, chosen for its sustainability. *Bound* and *trimmed* at Jackson House by **Quacks the Printer**, 7 Grape Lane, Petergate, York Yo1 7hu, T: +44 (0)1904 635967, info@quacks.info, www.radiusonline.info

contents

dedication 11

contents v

list of illustrations vi

acknowledgements ix

preface xi

INTRODUCTION in caps .... **xiii**

introduction xv

foreword *by Stephen Sayers* xvii

chapter one *Which was the first book in York?* 1

chapter two *the oldest extant book in York c.1020* 3

chapter three *other books and newspapers printed in York* ... 4

chapter four *early writing materials* 9

chapter five *the story of printing* 11

chapter six *the development of the printed word* 14

chapter seven *the work of the printer* 17

chapter eight *ink* 19

chapter nine *moveable type to computer graphics* 20

chapter ten *good page design* 22

chapter eleven *the next five hundred years* 25

chapter twelve *the imprints of the Jacksons* 29

appendix one *the York Pica* 33

appendix two *the longest line of craftsmen....* 45

appendix three *the Sessions Book Trust* 50

appendix four *What is the most readable typeface?* 58

appendix five *the quincentenary of book printing in York* ... 60

appendix six *quincentenary luncheon* 65

bibliography 69

index 70

list of illustrations in order of appearance

Front cover inspired by **Marc Chagall's lithograph**, 320mm x 420mm the lesson of *Philetas for Daphne et Chloe*, 1961, Paris, Biblioteque Nationale, the whole lithograph appears on prelim ii. Front flap photo: Martin Nelson and family Cathy, daughter Éilis and Muffin their dog. Colophon double page spread of the Sidney Sussex Pica, inside front cover. Facsimile of a **Jackson woodcut** *bowl of fruit,* , prelim i. In **Aloys Senefelder's** treatise he gives a practical indication of the range of results obtainable by the different lithographic modes and the possibilities of correction offered by resorting to several procedures. The plate is taken from an edition of the *Encyclopedia delle Arti Industrie*, published in Turin in 1885 by the Unione Tipographie, prelim ii. Front cover to the Supplement of the **Heath Family Engravers** 1779 to 1878, by John Heath prelim vi. **Pablo Picasso lithograph** for *le Chant des morts* by Pierre Reverley, 1948 320mm x 420mm, Pris, Biblioteque Nationale, prelim vi. **Georges Rouault lithograph**, *Autumn,* 1927-33, 570mm x 430mm, New York, Museum of Modern Art, prelim vii. Front cover of **Laurence Sterne** a life by Ian Campbell Ross, prelim x. **Annabel Kidston wood engraving,** *a traveller,* 1930, 155 x 230mm, prelim xii. **Henri Matisse lithograph,** *Odalisque in Dancing Girl's Trousers,* 1925, 440mm x 545mm Paris, Biblioteque Nationale, prelim xiii. **Georges Braque lithograph**, *Leaves, Colours, Light,* 1954, 600mm x

970mm, Milan, Fabio Castelli Collection, prelim xiv. **Alfred Sisley lithograph**, *the Riverside, or the Geese*, 1897, 320mm x 212mm, Paris, Bibliotheque Nationale, prelim xvi. **Guy Malet wood engraving,** *Sark girl,*1936, prelim xviii. **Eric Heckel lithograph,** *Handstand, 1916*, 196mm x 279mm, Munich, Staatliche Graphische Sammlung, prelim xviii. Two illustrations from the **Book of Kells,** page 1. Dust Wrapper of **The Bells and Bellringers of York Minster,** *by David Potter*, page 2. **Camille Pissarro lithograph**, *Women carrying Kindling Wood*, 1896, 300mm x 229mm, Berlin, Kupferstichkabinett, Staatliche Museen Preussischer Kulturbesitz, page 2. Illustration from the Gospel of Matthew, York Gospels; front cover of

the Gutenberg Galaxy by Marshall McLuhan; front cover of the Nature of the World, the Yorkshire Philosophical Society 1822-2000, by David Rubinstein page 3. A sermon printed by John Jackson in 1703 for the thanksgiving service of the Battle of Blenheim, page 4, Thomas Wanless York Minster Anthems printed by John Jackson in 1703, page 5. The York Gazetteer printed and published by John Jackson 1741, page 6. Yorkshire Philosphical Society proceedings printed by William Sotheran in 1865 for his uncle and in 1888 for the YPS, page 8. **Marini Marino lithograph**, *Acrobat, 1956,* 470mm x 625mm, Milan, Museo d'Arte Moderna; **Max Beckmann lithograph**, *Self- portrait with Cat and lamp*, 1920, 315mm x 470mm, Milan, Il Mercante di Stampe, page 10. **Maurice de Vlaminck lithograph**, *Bowl of Fruit*, 1921, 640mm x 475mm, Milan, Il Mercante di Stampe, page 13. Illustration of the wooden common press; **Max Ernst lithograph**, *Owl*, 1955, 362mm x 490mm, New York Museum of Modern Art, James Thrall Soby Fund, page 16. Common Press in use; Arab platen press at Jackson House in the bibliographic workshop, 1992, Sian Statters inspecting his work, Oliver Beckerlegge author of Weep Not for Me, a list of poetical epitaphs, published by Quacks Books, Graham Parry, page 18. Printers inc Poster, page 19; **Kauffer E Mcnight lithograph**, *poster praising the dynamics of flight,* 1918, Centro Documentazione Mondadori; Scholar Printer John Mason's indenture as an apprentice compositor, page 21. Front cover of **John Bromyard on Church and State,** *by Keith Walls*, printed by Quacks 2009, page 22. Marriage sheet for Kathy Worsley printed letterpress by Morleys, with outside diestamping by Sessions, 1961; Heath engraving catalogue printed by Quacks in the 1990s, page 24. **Pablo Picasso lithograph**, *the Bull eleventh and final state*, 1945, first drawn at the printers Mourlot reduced to its final eleventh state of a few lines, page 25.**Fernand Leger lithograph,** *Cyclist*, plate VII of *Cirque*, 1950; **Maurice Denis**, *On the Pale Silver Sofa*, 1898, 285mm x 401mm, New York, Brooklyn Museum and *the Reflections in the Fontain*, 1897, 240mm x 400mm, New York, Museum of Modern Art, page 27. Edith Sessions my grandmother, attendance's record at York Musical Society's rehearsals, printed by Henry Morley at Jackson House, Petergate, York, March 20th 1912, page 28. **Maurice Denis,** *the Reflections in the Fountain,* 1897, 240 x 400mm, New York, Museum of Modern Art, purchase fund, page 31. **Keith Walls** reading the Pica, page 43. Front cover of Drawing from Line to Life, by Mike Sibley, Quacks Books, 2008; Jackson House in the time of the Morleys, 1890s, page 46. The board of Directors of Quacks most exotic meeting, Raffles Garden, Singapore, Michael, Tim, Sue and Jo Sessions, page 47. Richard Cousans, production manager, fortieth birthday celebration at **Mandy O'Sullivan's** house, January 2010, Mandy O'Sullivan, Horst Meyer, Lesley Seeger, Michael Sessions, Richard Cousans, Andrew Leathley, Nathan Tate and Laura Anderson, Eilidh Newton, Sylvia Meyer. Some of us worked at Quacks, page 48. Recent photograph taken in the Bibliographic workshop at Jackson House Horst Meyer, Michael Sessions, Rachel Hopkins, Martin Nelson, Jackie Coverdale; A recently unearthed Jackson imprint, page 49. **The River Foss**, by *Michael Fife and Peter Walls;* **Badgers of Yorkshire & Humberside**, by *R. J. Paget* & *A. L. V. Middleton*, page 50; **Printing in York**, by *William K. & E. Margaret Sessions;* **A Wood in Ascam**, edited by *Alastair Fitter & Clifford Smith*, **York 1831-1981**, edited by *C. H. Feinstein,* **Essays in Quaker History** by *David Rubinstein*, page 53; **The Almshouses of York**, by *Carole Smith*, **Faith and Practice at a Quaker School** by *Graham Ralph,* page 54; **Reassuring 18th Century Protestants**, by *Arthur Holroyd*, **Great Lives**, edited by *Elaine Phillips and Michael Sessions*, **Friends and Comrades**, by *Sergei Nikitin*, **All is one Love**, by *Stephen Sayers*, illustrated by *Swea Sayers*, page 57; Photo of **John Woodcock**, **Matt Clark** looking on as **Mike Gowling** photos Keith Walls reading the Pica, page 61, Photo of the return of the Pica **Nicholas Rogers**, **Michael Sessions**, Bernard Barr, Keith Walls, Lesley Seeger, Gillian Holmes, Yumi Chapman, Margaret Grandidge, Brian Colton, Philip Chapman, Bill Sessions, Horst Meyer, Philip Achurch and Terry Casey, page 68; Flyer for Jackson Imprint monograph printed in 2004 for our 300th anniversary; flyer for Waddleton project; Radius front cover; Valentine Day, dry point intaglio etching printed at Quacks, January 2010, by Lesley Seeger, inside back cover. **Marc Chagall lithograph,** *Arabian Nights (plate 1),* 1948, New York, Museum of Modern Art, back cover. Reverse flap photo: Four Sessions family generations - Tim, Seb, Bill, Michael Sessions.

acknowledgements

Stephen Sayers for writing the foreword. He became Head of the School of Social Sciences and Associate Dean of the Faculty of Arts and Society at Leeds Beckett University. Stephen has served as an Ambassador of The Peace Museum in Bradford, and as a Governor of Friends' School, Great Ayton in North Yorkshire, The Mount and Bootham Schools and The Retreat in York. He is a Fellow of the Royal Society of Arts. He writes every morning.

Bernard Barr retired *sub librarian York Minster Library* for pointing us in the right direction to find more Jackson Imprints.

Linden Richardson and his father for letting us purchase their **Albion** *metal hand press*.

Nicholas Rogers, archivist of **Sidney Sussex College**, Cambridge for his help in *digitising* the only complete copy of the *Pica, Directorium Sacerdotum* the first book to be printed in York 18th February 1509/10 and arranging its loan so that it could be in York close to where it was printed on the 18th February 2010.

Robert McClements CEO of Print Yorkshire for his help with the chapter on the future and the planning of the exhibition and the celebrations around the 18th February 2010.

Bill Morrell for asking **Bill Sessions** to research the history of printing in York with **Margot Sessions**, which lead in 1972 to the purchase of the print business whose line of craftsmen can trace their pedigree from just after the close of the **seventeenth century** to the present day.

John Smart, who was responsible for the printing section of the science museum. He originated much of the text of the 1992 exhibition edition of *A Story of the Book* chapters 5, 7 and 8.

Keith Walls for writing the appendix on the **York Pica** and his constant enthusiasm for the quincentenary celebrations.

John King trustee and son of the co-founder for condensing fifty five years of minutes of **the Sessions Book Trust** to create an appendix on the Trust.

The staff and directors of **Quacks the Printer**, the successors to this *inheritance* who continue to practise many of the techniques past down to them by former colleagues using today's technology and for their help in the preparation of this book. It is a pleasure to work with them.

The trustees, past and present, of the **John Jackson** Trust for their help over the last 34 years.

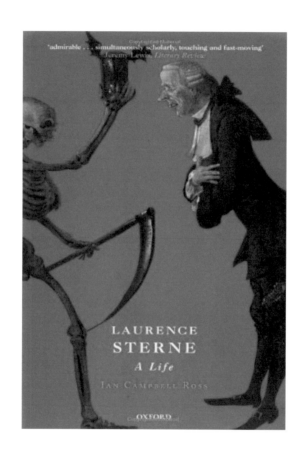

'admirable . . . simultaneously scholarly, touching and fast-moving'
Jeremy Lewis, Literary Review

LAURENCE
STERNE
A Life

IAN CAMPBELL ROSS

OXFORD

preface

This story of the book starts with the **Phoenicians** who had the perspicacity to form a 22 letter alphabet, before anyone else. It ends in the middle of the twenty first century where printers will be printing **electronic** parts as well as their more normal stock in trade, **books**.

Along the way there are glimpses of how the first printed book in York came about, *read* **Keith Walls** *appendix one*. We question who might have printed the **first English modern novel**, *read chapter 12*. The impact that moveable type had on the enlightenment is discussed in chapter six. Lithographic prints by **Picasso, Chagall** and a host of others enliven the text.

However, the best quote should be left for the preface. Some friends were kind enough to discuss with me in **Vahe's** the impact that moveable type had had on the world. **Matt Clark** of the Press and **John Woodcock** of the Yorkshire Post had asked me the question earlier in the day. David Miller the editor of the U3A newsletter summed it up. *Without the invention of* moveable type *the world wide net would not have been thought of.*

I believe that without **moveable type** the events of 1688 and 1704 would not have led to *religious toleration* and *parliamentary democracy* spreading from our shores across the **educated world**.

The book is factual but has some anecdotes for those that **enjoy stories**. This third edition includes a little about **ink** and **the Sessions Book Trust**. An extant **Jackson Imprint** dated before the turn of the seventeenth into the eighteenth century is still not found.

INTRODUCTION

TO DEMONSTRATE TO YOU THE READER, THAT CAPITALS ARE NOT THAT EASY TO READ WE HAVE SET THIS PAGE TWICE. ONCE IN CAPITALS USING A SANS SERIF EMBOLDENED TYPEFACE WHICH HAS NO SHADING.

xiv

introduction

We have set this introduction in the lower case using a serif face that employs shading (see page 23).

Page design and readability decisions of our authors are important. CAPITAL letters **interrupt the flow of reading** due to their similarity and lack of descenders and ascenders. Lower case is easier to read than upper. A capital letter is used where there is a change of sense at the beginning of a sentence. We believe that the use of CAPITALS anywhere else interrupts flow and readability. However, it is **grammatically correct** to start a *proper name* or noun with a **capital** or *upper-case letter*.

In the days of the **typewriter** there were two ways to <u>emphasise</u> words, <u>underlining</u> or the use of capitals. **<u>Compositors</u>** looked askance as descenders were cut <u>through</u> by the underline. We have given you our <u>thoughts</u> on <u>capitals</u> above. **Typographers**, on the other hand knew they could emphasise with the use of the **bold face,** by *italicising*, or by reducing the point size to eight point or increasing it to fourteen point**.**

Up until the 1970s all printed **readable pages** were controlled by a few apprenticed trained **compositors** who worked to strict *typographical rules* handed down by generation after generation of *craftsmen*. These rules have largely **never** been learnt by the *modern author* who is usually in charge of determining the typographical detail of the printed page.

Please enjoy reading about these important rules that this *style book* explains as you find out more about **the story of the book**.

foreword

It is a privilege to commend this book to readers. What is before you is a fascinating collection of material relating to the craft of printing. It contains a section on the history of printing, mainly in York and Yorkshire, along with how the printed word has evolved from its early beginnings and how printed publications are best presented to modern readers.

Printed style is key to this end, and the book considers paper, ink, serifs, shading and how to achieve effective page design. In part, the recommendations made are pertinent to printing generally, but the house style of Quacks Books is given precedence and is set out in detail. These clear guidelines should be a boon for authors submitting manuscripts for publication.

The book is well-illustrated, with various examples of printed work. There are lithographs, etchings, engravings and woodcuts by Max Ernst, Marc Chagall, Henri Matisse, Pablo Picasso, Georges Braque, and others. Lesley Seeger selected the illustrations, and examples of her work are also included.

In an Appendix to the main text, Keith Walls has provided a scholarly account of the York Pica, an ecclesiastical calendar informing priests about the dates of saints' days and their feasts. Hugo Goes printed it in the early sixteenth century, and it's the oldest complete surviving book printed in York using moveable type.

Quacks Books is the modern face of a venerable tradition. It can trace its roots back to 1703. In a second Appendix, the book traces the firm's direct, unbroken lineage in York to John Jackson in the early eighteenth century. This impressive pedigree may represent northern England's longest continuous line of craft printers. The present premises of Quacks Books in Grape Lane bear its founder's name, Jackson House.

During its history, this direct line of printers was associated with many noteworthy publications. Perhaps the most remarkable of these is the printing of the first two volumes of Laurence Sterne's nine-volume modern novel Tristram Shandy in 1760. Its distinction as the first novel ever published in England is celebrated as a major event in the history of literature. It was probably printed in Jackson House by John, the son of John Jackson.

A third Appendix deals with the Sessions Book Trust, established in 1967 by the Sessions, a York Quaker family. Its purpose is to promote the publication of books, booklets and pamphlets about Quaker values and history, as well as items about the history and natural history of York and its region. The present chairman of the Trust is Michael Sessions, a Director of Quacks Books.

The Directors and staff of Quacks Books have continued to develop the printing and publishing business in York. In 2000, they acquired Radius, a publishing company that produced a monthly directory of businesses in Yorkshire. The activities of what is now Radius Publishing Ltd. have expanded to include a wide range of publications, reaching an estimated quarter million readers. Its Managing Director is Martin Nelson, another Director of Quacks.

The future of Quacks is in no doubt. The introduction of digital technology has improved efficiency and expanded possibilities for both printing and publication. The Directors, Martin Nelson, Lesley Seeger and Michael Sessions, have been joined by Jackie Coverdale, administration and Rachel Hopkins, the design team. The team is justifiably proud of their company's past and present capabilities.

May their vision and sense of adventure help continue to bring a publishing Renaissance in York and beyond.

chapter one

Which was the first book in York?

Paulinus and **James** the Deacon who both preached *christianity* in 627 a.d. and who founded the Minster School, would have owned a *bible* for their missionary work. The first record documents Wilfrid's presentation to the minster c.700 a.d. of a two volume copy of the *gospels* written in letters of gold on purple parchment and illuminated.

The supreme example of celtic illumination written on the island of Iona in the second half of the eighth century was the **Book of Kells**. The *illustration* shows the opening words of **Matthew** 1:18. The book is kept in **Trinity College Library**, Dublin.

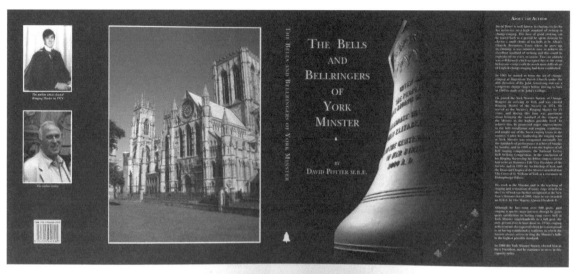

chapter two

the oldest extant book in York c.1020

The **York Gospels** has been used as an oath book for nearly a thousand years and is still used at the enthronement of each archbishop.

The book has survived as it was not always kept in the **Minster Library** or with the archives.

The library was burnt down in 1069. The **Minster Treasury**, in which the gospels volume was then kept, was plundered in 1547.

The book was removed during the commonwealth, but returned in 1668.

It is currently kept in the **Minster Library** where a *facsimile* edition may be seen by visitors.

Jackson house has a similar *facsimile* edition of the *York Gospels*.

  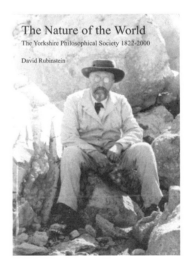

chapter three

other books and newspapers printed in York

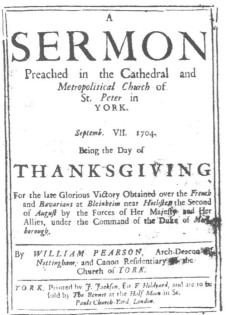

York is believed to be the third provincial centre to commence printing after **Caxton** began printing in Westminster in 1476. The first book printed in York in 1509/10 by **Hugo Goes** (pronounced Goose) in Steengate (Stonegate) was entitled the *Pica or Directorium Sacerdotum*.

The book is an ecclesiastical calendar which gives the dates for the various saints' days and other Christian festivals in each year from 1497 to 2011. The pica is 256 pages long; size is 160mm x 95mm. It is section sewn and bound in full leather.

Sidney Sussex College in Cambridge has the only substantially complete copy. It has one leaf missing which is most likely to be blank. **York Minster Library** has an incomplete copy that has the last twenty-six pages missing including the colophon.

In 1642, on the eve of the civil war, **Charles I** stayed in York for 5 months and the king's printer **Robert Barker** set up his wooden press in **St. William's College**. Amongst others he printed the *Proclamation forbidding all Levies of Forces without His Majesties expresse pleasure, signified under His Great seale, and all Contributions of Assistance to any such Levies.*

Some forty years later **John White,** in 1688, printed the proclamation for **William of Orange** to succeed to the english throne. He was imprisoned in **Hull** jail for sedition until the **Duke of Marlborough** rode out to meet and join the future, **King William.** He had been instructed by **James II** to repulse him. **James** fled to **France** never to return. The right of parliament to make law, written into **William's** proclamation subsequently became law. The *divine right* of the English *Kings* ended and *Lockean political philosophy* influenced the emerging liberal parliamentary systems of the modern civilised world.

In 1703 **John White's** apprentice **John Jackson** printed on his own account a book of anthems for **Thomas Wandlass**, organist to the cathedral of York. **John Jackson** who was born in 1678 was twenty-five. Three generations of the **Jackson family** were to remain printing in **Grape Lane** and **Petergate** until 1790. The Jacksons counted amongst their customers **Laurence Sterne,** who was the author of *Tristram Shandy*, purported to be the *first english modern novel.*

York's first newspaper was the *York Mercury*, published in 1718-19, a single sheet seven inches by five and half inches costing one and a half d., printed by Grace White in Coffee Yard.

The **Jacksons** were to print the *York Gazetteer,* a weekly newspaper, for around ten years in the 1740s. In its opening issue it printed, *As this paper is partly set on foot, to correct the weekly poison of the* **York Courant,** it declared, *tis hoped that the well wishers to the cause of liberty and Protestantism will give it encouragement.* The only existing paper at that time influenced by two physicians, Dr John Burton and Dr Francis Drake had Jacobite sympathies, supporting arbitrary power and Roman Catholicism. **Laurence** and his uncle **Jacque Sterne** edited the *York Gazetteer* which took the more liberal less authoritarian view, but despite this the Tories wished to nobble this liberal attempt to publish. Mr Fox a Tory was asked to assault John Jackson and Laurence Sterne. Laurence remembered these characters when he wrote his novel **Tristram Shandy** some

Full Anthems, AND Verse Anthems,

As they are Ordered by the Dean and Chapter, to be Sung in the Cathedral and Metropoliticall Church of St. Peters in York, Collected by Thomas Wanless, Batchelor of Musick, and Organist there.

YORK.
Printed by John Jackson, for and Sold by Thomas Baxter, Book-Seller in Peter-Gate, York.
1703.

few years later. Luckily Sterne was not in the **Petergate/Grape Lane office** at the time. John Jackson took the *Tory* Mr **Fox,** the coal merchant, to court as he nearly succeeded in halting this *liberal* attempt to publish. The *Tory was* bound over to keep the peace and the freedom of the *liberal* press was retained.

In the nineteenth century the **Jacksons'** successor, **William Sotheran,** sometimes with the collaboration of his uncle **John Sotheran,** the bookseller, printed, in 1822 the proceedings of the newly formed *Yorkshire Philosophical Society.* Amongst their members were the York City Treasurer **Robert Davies** who was to itemise in 1868, all the known imprints of the eighteenth century York Printers in a book entitled *a Memoir of the York Press.* Davies numbered some eighteen **Jackson** imprints, not including the hundreds of editions of the York Gazetteer that came from this press. The Radius magazine and Quacks Books are still printing today in **Grape lane** and **Petergate**, albeit with different craftsmen involved.

In the twentieth century the three generations of **Morleys**, successors to **William Sotheran,** (whose family ran bookshops in **Sackville Street**, off Park lane in **London** and **York**) printed the *wedding service programme* for the future Duchess of Kent, **Kathy Worsley** who lived at **Hovingham Hall** and was married in 1963 in **York Minster.**

The **Morleys** were to continue to print the weekly service sheet for the **Minster** and all **York Theatre Royal** programmes. **Michael Sessions** remembers in the 1960s, when he might have been 14 years old, accompanying his father **Bill Sessions** to investigate the *Morley passage,* off **Petergate** and climbing the stairs to **Mrs Morley's** first floor office. They could hear the familiar sound of the feed system of a *Heidelberg automatic* *platen* in the background. Its repetitive on/off suction of the paper as it is taken from the in tray to the platen to be printed and then released to the out tray. **Mrs Morley** was reading a proof and was singularly unimpressed by this visit of two enquiring printers. I am glad though that I met her. She had trained as a teacher and after marrying one of the twin **Morley** grandsons of **Valentine Morley**, who had taken over from **William Sotheran,** she ran a well-respected printing firm with the practical help of her husband and his twin brother.

In 1972 **Morleys** was again printing for the *Yorkshire Philosophical Society*, this time the one hundred and fifty annual proceedings of this august society which that year had a gold cover.

In 1972 largely for historic reasons, **Bill Sessions** bought into the **Morley** company and became chairman with his son **Michael Sessions** becoming the managing director. In the next fifty years, **Quacks** as it was renamed, printed and published in six volumes for **Cambridge University Library** a list of all the colour plate books donated by **Norman Waddleton,** firstly to his old college **Emmanuel** known as the *Waddleton* Collection; the third volume of a trilogy of books cataloguing and illustrating the *Heath Engravings* whose almost complete collection of *Heath wood and steel engravings* has ended up in the **Morrell library** at York University in the *special collections* thanks to the generosity of **John and Patricia Heath** of Bath with their link to the University of York after becoming customers of **Quacks** in the 1980s.

In 2000 **Quacks** bought the rights to continue to print and now publish the monthly publication known as the **Radius**. The **Radius** acted as a rural Yellow Pages to businesses and private homes. The **radius** has now expanded reaching an estimated monthly readership of perhaps a quarter of a million readers.

The Sessions Book Trust was set up by Michael's father **Bill Sessions** and aunt **Anne King** in 1967 to part sponsor scripts wishing to be published. Since my father's death in 2013 The Sessions Book Trust has been administered from Jackson House, 7 Grape Lane, Petergate, York Yo1 7hu and can be contacted at info@quacks.info. In the last fifty-five years the Trust has contributed to somewhere around 800 books that have been published on subjects including the arts, natural history, Quakerism, York and Yorkshire.

At the time of the quincentenary *the History of the Bell Ringers and Bells of York Minster,* which is profusely illustrated in full colour with the older photographs being in black and white, was published. It is some 154 pages long, size 290 mm x 225mm printed litho, using the book face **Baskerville,** section sewn and hard bound with dust wrapper. It is available through all good bookshops by quoting the Quacks Books isbn 978-1-904446-20-0 or from the Author **David Potter**, Minster Yard, York or **Quacks Books**, 7 Grape Lane, Petergate, York.

More recently in 2018 Quacks Books has published Great Lives, in a hard back and soft back edition. It traces the lives of thirty Bootham School, York Old Scholars and how they made a difference.

This year 2023 we are hard at work on various projects. We are putting together the first of a number of volumes of a Thematic Catalogue of the known works of Franz Liszt; a publication recognising the role of Bretton Hall and its contribution to the arts; and we also look forward to assisting Bootham School in printing a commemorative book, celebrating their bicentenary.

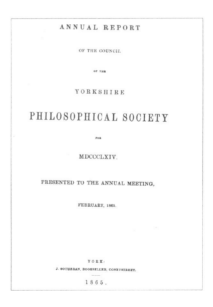

chapter four

early writing materials

The **Egyptians** used *papyrus* between three and nine hundred years before the birth of **Christ**.

Two hundred years before Christ the manufacture of *parchment* was perfected at **Pergamum** in Asia Minor.

In one hundred and five years anno domini **Ts'ai Lun,** a mandarin at the imperial court of China, invented paper. He mixed *worn-out hempen sandals*, *fishing nets and old rags, the inner bark of trees* and *water*.

One thousand years after its invention *paper* reached **Europe** by a series of coincidences. In seven hundred and fifty-one the Muslim Governor of **Samarkand**, whilst repulsing an attack on the city, is reported to have taken twenty thousand **Chinese** Prisoners, some of them adept in the art of *papermaking*. From **Samarkand** the knowledge of *papermaking* spread to the Middle East: **Baghdad, Damascus, Tiberias, Hamah, Tripoli** and later **Cairo** became important manufacturing centres. In the twelfth century the **Moors** introduced *paper* to **Spain** and **Sicily**. In 1492 the **Muslim Moors** lost Spain, hence the art of *papermaking* passed into the hands of less skilled **Christian** Craftsmen and almost immediately the quality of *paper* declined. In the following centuries the manufacture of *paper* established itself in Europe. The manufacturing process remained basically the same until the nineteenth century when, once again for economic reasons, the spread of education caused a sudden increase in demand for printed knowledge. *Wood* was introduced as a substitute for *linen*. In the early part of the twentieth century *paper makers* had not learnt to balance the *pH* or acidity of the wood-based *paper*. This led to the ageing or yellowing of popular *paper backs* such as the early **Penguin** books. By the latter part of the twentieth century *paper* had been balanced. This means that modern *book printing paper* is neither acidic or caustic, unlike their earlier *wood-based paper* uncles and aunts.

chapter five

the story of printing

The first **prints** were made in **China** in the fifth century anno domini using *wooden blocks* carved with the characters of the Chinese language.

By 1407 the **Koreans** were making small *metal types* for use in printing and the technique of *block printing* had spread to Europe.

In the middle of the fifteenth century **Johannes Gutenberg**, working in Mainz, invented the european method of printing using separate *metal types*, a *wooden press* and an oil-based *ink*.

In 1476 **Caxton** began work in Westminster. Later printing spread to **Oxford (1478), St Albans (1479/80)** and **York (1509/10).**

The *wooden press* was little changed in design until the late eighteenth century when attempts were made to improve it, without success. The first all *iron hand press* soon replaced the old wooden design. The **Albion** press situated in the comp room at **Jackson House** was made in 1822.

In 1814, the Times newspaper was printed on a steam driven machine press invented by Koenig and Bauer in 1811. From this point presses began to be designed for particular work, such as printing newspapers, books or packaging. The *iron hand press* was still being used in the twentieth century for proofing and smaller work.

At the end of the eighteenth century a new system of printing called *lithography* was invented by **Senefelder**. A picture drawn in greasy crayon on a stone could produce a print if the stone were first dampened with water and then inked with greasy ink.

The ink would stick only to the crayon marks and would be repelled by the damp stone. At first used mainly for pictures, the lithographic process began to be used for other purposes and by 1980 *modern offset lithography* had almost completely supplanted printing from metal type or a relief plate for most processes in most countries.

Fox Talbot's development of the *positive/negative method of photography* led him to try to apply this to *printing* and after years of experimentation by many people a successful method of *translating photographs* into *printing plates* was developed in the 1880's.

Many attempts were made to speed up the process of *typesetting* during the early years of the nineteenth century, but it was not until 1886, when the *Linotype* was designed by **Merganthaler**, that a really successful machine was produced. In 1897 another typesetting system *Monotype,* was invented by **Lanston** and these two *hot-metal* composers dominated the field for the next sixty years, the *Linotype* being favoured by newspaper printers and the *Monotype* by book printers.

During a similar period, 1880 to 1897, a Czech, **Karl Klic**, worked on another new method of printing, *photogravure.* In this process the lights and darks of a picture are represented by shallower or deeper pits in a metal surface; when a liquid ink washes over the plate and the surface is wiped clean the ink is retained in the pits and will print light or dark tones on to paper. At first *photogravure* was only used for fine art pictures but it was used to print a newspaper and widely used for such things as mass circulation magazines and mail order catalogues before *web offset* took over for all but the longest runs.

In the mid 1950's the first machines to set text using photographic negatives and a camera instead of *hot-metal* and *moulds* were introduced and gradually the *photo setters* have taken over from the *hot-metal* machines. The introduction of computers to assist in this text setting process led to further rapid developments. By the late 1970's text characters and pictures could be translated into electronic impulses (*digitisation*) and it became possible to assemble a complete page of text and pictures electronically, changing the design until the best result was obtained; a printout would be produced from which a printing plate could be made.

By the turn of the twenty first century *computer to plate* machines were being installed by most *litho* printing houses. This allowed *digitised* information to be placed directly onto a polyester or metal litho printing plate.

This technology was further developed to take digitised information direct to the printing cylinder of the press. This created the *digital* printing press. Some digitised presses used ink others used toner. Both processes continued to use paper; however it is perfectly possible to print by *litho* on a variety of synthetic materials such as *polyester* or *acetate*.

Apple Mackintosh worked in the 1980s with **Adobe** to produce a *graphics computer* which has dominated the printing industry ever since. **Adobe** software programmes *illustrator, photoshop* and *indesign* (formerly *pagemaker*) have allowed *digitised typefaces* to retain the benefits of **readability** created by *shading, serifs* and the occasional use of *italics* and **bold** whilst using the more readable *lower case*. The *upper case* being left for stone masons and interrupting the readers flow at the beginning of sentences and the beginning of proper names. One of the disadvantages of these multi-effect software packages is that the look of the page has become king and the readability of the page almost forgotten. **Jackson House's** *style* thinks that **readability** should be the guiding principle.

chapter six

the development of the printed word

The **written word** in the form in which we know it, where a letter represents a sound, was developed by the **Phoenicians** and formed their greatest *gift* to the **Greeks**, who by circa seven hundred years before Christ were using this twenty-two sound alphabet. This was a major improvement, when one considers that the Egyptians pictorial or hieroglyphic writing was composed of over *one thousand* and *thirty* characters – was slow to write – and difficult to learn. The twenty-two sound alphabet soon became expanded by two vowels to the twenty-four letter Greek Alphabet and later to the modern twenty-six letter alphabet.

Following the collapse of the Roman Empire, culture and civilisation had been pushed to such remote places as Ireland and Christian Missions in **Lindsfarne** in the North quite close to **Newcastle**, where in the seventh century, anno domini, the characteristic **half uncial** handwriting was established. These missionaries soon became famed for their beautiful work and monasteries were established in other centres, including **York**. This **half uncial** script was the one *Alcuin* replaced with the neater and more fluent **Carolingian Miniscule**.

eboracum (Half-uncial)

eboracum (Carolingian Minuscule)

These **scribes** were not superseded in York, the *third earliest provincial printing centre* in England and the *first centre* north of Oxford until Monday the eighteenth of February 1509/10 when Hugo Goes set up as a *buke printer* using the new Gutenberg inspired *moveable* type.

Writing in 1962 *Marshall McLuhan* in the **Gutenberg Galaxy** discusses the impact that the advent of printing causes.

He quotes William Blake, Alexander Pope, John Ruskin, James Joyce, John Newton, Adam Smith, Dr Johnson, Burke, Hume, Reynolds, Kames, Wharton, Oliver Goldsmith, Francis Bacon, Edgar Allan Poe, Baudelaire, Valery, Leonardo de Vinci, T. S. Eliot, John Stuart Mill and Marconi.

He discusses the human impact of the change from working with hand tools such as the quill pen to a world of assembly lines; a world where the public and the market economy have given the reader the power to determine choice rather than the patron; and the move from a religious order based on myths to an appreciation that scientific rigour and experimentation can bring us much closer to the beauty and mystery of our natural world. He predicts that the twenty first century gods will be the sons of Marconi.

May we long remember the inheritance given to us by the printer/compositor especially remembering that we all have the freedom to get it right.

May we long remember the inheritance given to us by the printer/compositor especially remembering that we all have the freedom to get it right, and not use calibri.

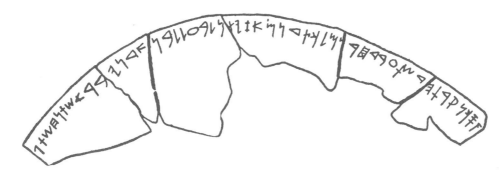

Phoenician inscription on a bronze bowl, about 950 b.c.

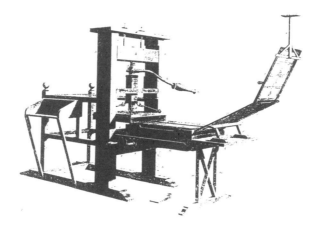

chapter seven

the work of the printer

The **book printer** often had to carry out all the tasks of *printing* himself, whereas in the nineteenth century in large printing shops various specialist workmen undertook each part of the process.

The first part of any job was to set the *text* with moveable lead *type*. The trays of metal *type* were kept in storage racks, and the trays of the particular style and size of **capitals** called *sort* to be used would be placed at the top and the case of small letters at the bottom. This is why the printer talks about *upper case* and *the lower case* instead of capitals and small letters.

Occasionally ***compositor printers*** felt rather *out of sorts* if a particular piece of moveable type was missing from that case. Also *apprentice compositors* had to be quite careful when selecting *their ps and qs* as they looked similar.

Even though moveable *type* was a **technological breakthrough** from the era of the scribe, the storage of standing *type* and the setting of moveable *type* seems to us so antiquated. Compare it with the ease of the computer and the sophisticated page design software programmes such as *indesign* of the twenty first century.

After all the text was set, the *type*, assembled on a long tray known as a *galley* would be taken to the hand press and one or two prints taken from it. These *galley proofs* would then be read carefully by the *reader* standing at the *reader's desk*. Any mistake was marked using a special code. *The compositor* would then correct the type, taking out the wrong characters and inserting the correct ones. He would usually do this standing at the *imposing stone*. The type would then be put into an iron frame – *a chase* – and wedged tightly into place with the aid of wooden spaces or *furniture*. It could then be taken to one of the hand presses for printing.

The ***Albion*** *hand press*, although it can be used by one man, usually had two people operating it, one man to ink the type with mushroom shaped leather balls. *He had to be a dab hand.* The other put clean paper in place and then pulled the lever to make the print. Working hard they might manage around two hundred to two hundred and fifty pulls an hour. *The **Arab** mechanical press* automatically *inks* the type and makes the impression. It requires only one man to operate and works much more quickly, as a printer just *treadled* the machine to keep the clam shaft opening and closing.

The printed sheets were often hung up on lines to dry. After this it would be necessary to trim the sheets with a hand guillotine. The book then depending on its size would either be stapled or stitched.

Finally the printer would have to wrap up the finished work ready for collection and take the chase of type to pieces, sorting the type back into their places in the type tray for use again.

chapter eight

ink

Ink, from Middle English ynke, from Old French enque, from Latin encaustum ("purple ink used by Roman emperors to sign documents"), from Ancient Greek ἔγκαυστον (énkauston, "burned-in"), from ἐν (en, "in") + καίω (kaíō, "burn").

What a wonderful English word.

Ink is a gel, sol, or solution that contains at least one colourant, such as a dye or pigment, and is used to colour a surface to produce an image, text, or design. Ink is used for drawing or writing with a pen, brush, reed pen, or quill. Inks are an essential part of the letterpress, lithographic, flexographic or silkscreen printing process.

Twenty Billion pounds of ink is consumed each year in this world, and if we all used a readable serif face typeface such as Baskerville as opposed to Calibri, we would reduce this expenditure by 20% to sixteen billion pounds saving 4 billion pounds per year.

In the middle of the 15th century, a new type of ink had to be developed for the printing press used by Johannes Gutenberg. Gutenberg's dye was indelible, oil-based, and made from the soot of lamps (lamp-black) mixed with varnish and egg white. Two types of ink were prevalent at the time: the Greek and Roman writing ink (soot, glue, and water) and the 12th century variety composed of ferrous sulphate, gall, gum, and water. Neither of these handwriting inks could adhere to printing surfaces without creating blurs. Eventually an oily, varnish-like ink was produced by heating and burning soot, turpentine, and walnut oil created specifically for the wooden printing press.

The first lithographic inks were composed of beeswax, tallow soap and lampblack. More recently UV light has been used to polymerise modern inks, so they are fixed instantaneously to the paper substrate. This allows for much faster printing speeds than hitherto.

chapter nine

moveable type to computer aided graphics

The *metal type* which all **printers** used until the middle of the twentieth century had remained unchanged in form from **Gutenberg's** day. The *stick shape* makes *type* easy to pick up, and a notch on one side tells the **compositor** which way up the character is without his having to look at it. It was **Gutenberg** who invented the method of making *type* by first preparing a hardened *steel punch* with the shape of the letter on the end, trimmed to fit into the bottom of a *mould* which was made in two halves. *Molten type metal* – a mixture of *lead, tin* and *antimony* – was then poured from a *ladel* into the top of the *mould* and the person called the **typecaster,** who held the *mould* in one hand

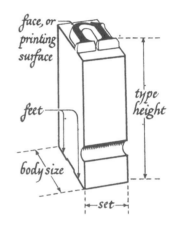

some of the more important parts of a piece of type

would jerk it upwards to force the *metal* into all parts of the *matrix*. The *metal* solidified almost at once and the *mould* could be opened, and the new *stick of type* ejected. When sufficient *types* of that character had been cast a new *matrix* would then be fitted, the *mould* halves sliding against each other to fit the width of the new *letter*. The newly *cast types* then had to have the *tang* of excess *metal* broken off and the bottom *planed* down, so they were all the correct height, *type high*.

All *type* was *hand-made* until about 1830 when *machines* which *cast type* were invented. The same principles were used but the *mould* opened and closed automatically and the *molten metal* was pumped instead of poured. The machines were called casters, had as many as ten thousand moving parts and were very noisy. Whilst they were totally *mechanical*, their **sophistication** predicted the *dawn* of a **nonmechanical logistics** just around the corner.

Later in **Victorian** times machines which set type by using a *keyboard* like a computer were invented *casting the type* as it was required. The **compositor** simply melted it down after use instead of having to labouriously sort it back into a *type case*.

the computer age

Desk top publishing finally saw the demise of the **compositor** in the latter part of the twentieth century and without knowing it we all became **page designers** with its subsequent consequences.

chapter ten

good page design

Presentation is important. We all learn more and feel generally uplifted when the printed page has been thoughtfully and well designed.

Winston Churchill said...

*The **printer** must put his **labour** and **materials** to the best possible use, in disseminating **knowledge** more widely, conveying **news** more speedily, expressing **information** more clearly, commemorating **events** more gracefully, and adorning life more beautifully.*

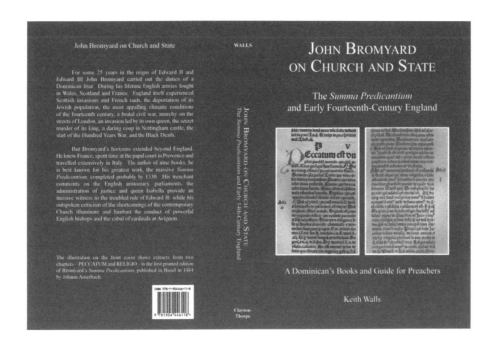

In this technological age the printed word remains the most versatile and permanent record, the most useful tool for reference, and communication. Since the first edition of *the story of the book* the internet has become a serious competitor. However, the book is still a very versatile form of communication. It is also true that good page design is as relevant for the net as it is for the printed page.

useful hints

Good sized **margins** help *readability*. The inner margin, the *gutter*, should be around half the outer margin, *the for-edge*, as on a double page spread there will always be two *gutter* margins. The top margin, *the head* should be bigger than the *gutter*. *The for-edge* margin should be bigger and the bottom page margin or *foot* should be the biggest. With a saddle stitched book, the gutter margin should increase by a millimetre every three or four double page spreads from the centre of the book, to cope with the extra thickness of the book. With a *perfect bound* book there should be a wider gutter margin so that the back of the book need not be broken open to read the words closest to the gutter margin.

Emboldened headings and even a few important **words** in the *text* contribute to understanding. *Italicising* terms or the *titles* of books can add to the interest of the **reader** and the *look* of the page. Capitals should be used in only two places as they are slower to read (see the introduction). A full stop ends the sentence with the next sentence beginning with a capital, to **interrupt** the *sense*. A **new sentence** will bring a further sense to the *text*. It is also grammatically correct to use a **capital** for a *proper noun*. For instance. *Michael Sessions*, *Grape Lane* or *York Minster*. In all other cases our **house style** does not use *capitals*.

shading and good letter form

Good **letter-form** cannot be *easily defined*, if indeed it can be *defined* at all. Other **arts**, under the scrutiny of generations of *critics*, have accumulated a **technique** and terminology of appraisal; the art of letter design has not. Certain **plain** virtues may, however, be described as essential to *good letters*.

The first of these is certainly the quality of **familiarity**. In overall **proportions**, in **thickness** of *stroke* and in shape of *outline*, every letter of a good **fount** must be similar, within reasonable limits, to the **form** of that *letter* to which **readers** are *accustomed*. The prime function of that **letter** is to *communicate* instantly, and any novelty of basic form may be a positive obstruction to *smooth reading* and even perhaps to **recognition**. Each letter, in fact, should be *distinct* from all the others, and capable of being *recognised* at a glance, but no **letter** should be so distinct as to attract more than a *glance*.

Shading is defined as the difference between the **thicker** and the *thinner* in the different **strokes** and the different parts of a stroke of a *letter*. **House style** would always recommend the use of a readable shaded serif face such as Baskerville. These faces use shading and serifs unlike Calibri and Arial. Calibri a sans serif faces is designed without shading or serifs. Whilst to the eye they look cleaner, the reader will spend longer distinguishing the sense with these faces as the different letters of the alphabet look more alike, and there are no serifs to guide the eye along the phrase or shading to help differentiate the individual letters.

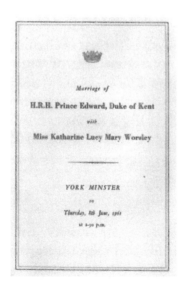

chapter eleven

the next five hundred years

digital printing

The new technology of printing is digital. The printing industry is possibly as much as 80% of the expanding industry of digital media. Print is the fifth largest employer in Yorkshire and Humberside employing eighteen thousand people and generating a sales total of some two billion pounds. As much as twenty percent of this is digital printing.

digital design

Computers have dominated typesetting since Apple brought out their first print related computer and Adobe designed

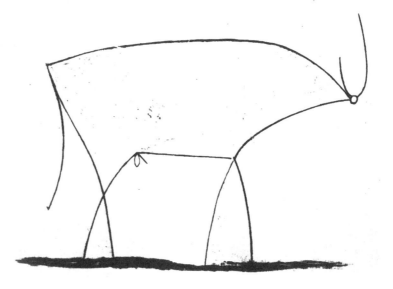

their page design software to power it. Images are digitally processed, and page design is created on screen. Digital technology improves the efficiencies of print, cutting waste and costs.

the web

The print industry has led the field in the amount of data that can be sent across the world wide web. High quality large pictures when turned into pixels may be as much as ten megabytes of information. If a book of two hundred and fifty colour illustrations is to be sent across the web then the average email size maximum of six megabytes is not enough.

However, file sharing websites such as wetransfer have grown up and can take a digital book of information of up to 100 megabytes or one hundred million bytes, an american billion.

imagine a world without print.

No explanations on your milk as to when it will remain fresh. No guidance on your prescription drug as to the frequency of dosage. Difficult to find out the date without a calendar on the wall or pocket diary. No posters, no books, no brand names on a product, no helpful information delivered by the post office to select post code areas, like the Radius Mags printed at Quacks each month and used by a potential readership of a quarter of a million people.

sustainability

Paper has become a recycled product especially where two soft wood trees are planted for everyone felled. In anno domini one hundred and five it was made from, amongst other things, hempen sandals and the woods remained untouched until the nineteenth century.

printed paper circuit boards

Print Yorkshire gained funding to create a paper printed circuit board. The future of print in Yorkshire and elsewhere is only limited by our current imagination. The future will be bright for those of us with lateral thinking like **Print Yorkshire** who spend their time promoting Yorkshire print and amongst others, **Quacks Books** ready to advise you on your next book.

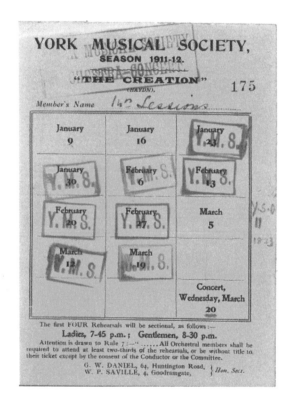

chapter twelve

the imprints of the Jacksons, who flourished from 1703 to 1790 in Grape Lane and Petergate, York

There are copies of the Jacksons' work in many of the university libraries around the world.

The **oldest extant work** is a volume of *anthems* put together by **Thomas Wanlefs** the organist at York Minster in 1703. The only copy that is known is in New York Public Library. Page size 155mm x 80mm, 62 pages, with a page addendum of a list of preachers at the Cathedral of St Peters, in York, section sewn with card cover printed in black.

Jackson in 1704 printed a sermon of some 32 pages page which was section sewn. The Jackson house copy is bound with another sermon and cased in a quarter bound leather binding with marbled boards. There are other copies in York Minster Library, Cambridge College Libraries, the Bodleian, a number of libraries in America, other European Countries and Australia. The sermon was giving thanks for the victory at the battle of Blenheim (*Blindheim*) over the French and Bavarians. It has been said that as a result of this victory, the first defeat the French had incurred since Louis XIV came to the throne in 1645 allowed the ideas of John **Locke** and William **Penn** to become more prominent first in England and then in the rest of the world.

The toleration of other peoples' religions or sects of a religion, such as the Quakers and parliamentary democracy as opposed to the divine right of kings and dictators has spread through most of the civilised and educated world.

Blenheim changed the axis of power and led to a more liberal approach. Jackson also printed secular works. The Bodleian in Oxford holds a copy of the *Catalogus Pharmocorum* printed in 1707, A list of medicines that the eighteenth-century pharmacist might stock. Page size –150 x 70–mm 230 pages, section sewn with card cover.

In 1740 the Jacksons started the York Gazetteer a newspaper that was distributed to many parts of

Yorkshire. Its editor was none less than the future author of *Tristram Shandy,* Laurence Sterne whose uncle Jacque Sterne was the current Precentor at York and one of the leaders of the local Whigs. He lived at **Grays Court** where we lunched on the 18th February 2010 to celebrate the **quincentenary** of printing in York. There is a story well documented as it reached a court of law where the Tory Mr Garbutt tried to nobble John Jackson to stop this liberal newspaper reaching its readers. Jackson having defended himself sent word to Sterne to stay in his parish at Sutton on the Forest until the Tory was arrested.

It is known that the first two volumes of *Tristram Shandy* were printed in York. However, there is no imprint as it is thought that Sterne wanted his readers to assume it was printed in London. Is it unlikely that **Laurence Sterne** would have used another York printer than Jackson after **Jackson** had defended his right to publish? *Tristram Shandy*, his first novel has been said to be the **first english modern novel.**

It is certain that John Jackson junior printed the *rebellion* for the volunteer **James Ray** of Whitehaven in Cumbria. The book gives a first-hand account of **James Ray's** experiences in putting down this rising of the Scots who wished a Catholic King. Page size 103 mm x 165 mm, octavo, 10 prelims, 451 pages, plus a frontispiece and a note from the author at the back with wood cuts typical to **Jackson**, section sewn with drawn on cover printed in one colour black. The book went to many editions. Other editions were printed in Bristol. The book is held in many libraries around the world including the Minster and Carlisle Library. A private copy was bought for sixty pounds by **Bill Sessions** in 1997. It can be seen that the Jackson flourish of a basket of fruit used on the half title page of this book prelim (i) was used not only by **John Jackson** junior but his son **Francis Jackson.**

Francis Jackson produced quite some work for the courts and the theatre. He produced the Poll Book for members in Parliament to represent the City of York 10th October 1774.

His Father, **John Jackson**, had produced a similar book for the election in 1758 and his Father, **John Jackson Senior** had produced a Poll Book for the 1741 election.

Francis Jackson's *Animadversions of an Hour, outline of the Oliverium Spirit of Usuration examin'd* with a word or two to Melchizedech has been compared favourably with his contemporary's John Baskerville's work. Our house style typeface is **Baskerville.**

The total number of extant Jackson imprints is approaching fifty if one counts the fifteen-year run of the *York Gazetteer* as one. If you included each extant edition of the *Gazetteer* it would increase to hundreds.

These imprints give an indication of the kind of secular and religious work that the Jacksons, this eighteenth century printer, situated quite close to the south door of the cathedral, would have been involved. It is hoped that more imprints will come to light as more people help in this research project. **Plomer** has two **Jackson imprints**, Davies has eight. The 2004 Quacks publication of the Jackson imprints revealed thirty- five. The extant imprints currently are approaching fifty.

These imprints were all printed in Grape Lane and Petergate on wooden hand presses. The present composing room at Jackson house shows a printing workshop using moveable type and metal hand presses that were in use from the beginning of the nineteenth century. It is hoped that a wooden common press will be built in York so that the first three hundred years of printing in York can be more adequately demonstrated.

Appendix One

The York Pica of 18th February 1510

Over the decades and centuries each major ecclesiastical foundation in Catholic Europe, whether religious or secular, built up its own body of practice for the daily worship of God which was – and is – the primary purpose of its existence. Such usage, gradually developed over long periods, doubtless modified – for example as to the timing of services – and perhaps influenced by nearby or powerful institutions came to be codified into texts to which were given such titles as, *Ordinale, Custumarium, Directorium* or *Consuetudinarium*.

In this western, Catholic Church, the prominence of Rome exerted a widespread dominance, but geography, slow communications and local pride ensured throughout the medieval period, that regional variety continued to flourish. This rich diversity of usage is most easily discerned in the *kalendars* which preface most liturgical book: so missals and breviaries surviving in a fragmentary condition can often be identified as to their origin by the presence in the *kalendar* of saints venerated in a certain area.

In England it was not the Use of Canterbury which was followed, as a model for the parish churches within its large province, since Canterbury was a monastic church. Instead, it was the secular cathedral of Salisbury whose practices were adhered to by some five or six thousand parish churches in the South and Midlands. This guide is known as the Sarum. Hereford too had its special Use: but throughout the greater part of the Northern Province it was the example of York which provided the form of worship for the days, weeks and seasons of the Church year.

Differences, then, existed: but common to all the secular churches was the established sequence of daily services. Matins and Lauds, usually combined, began early, round daybreak. Mass was celebrated about eleven o'clock: and the final offices were Vespers and Compline in the late evening. This was the norm for parish churches. Cathedrals followed a richer programme, including the lesser offices of Prime, Terce, Sext and None.

A time traveller finding him-or herself in one of the larger York churches in fifteen hundred – St. Martin's, Coney Street, All Saints Pavement, St Olave's, Marygate or St. Michael's, Spurriergate – would notice several differences from modern worship in either of these churches. The priest spoke in Latin : not always audibly: often with his back to the congregation. Images abounded, the thurifer made liberal use of incense and many parishioners came late into the Mass, often just in time to witness the Elevation of the Host. Other masses might be being conducted simultaneously at side altars by one or two chantry priests. At less solemn, less dramatic moments of the Mass many parishioners, unable to understand Latin and illiterate in English, would be gossiping among themselves.

The most obvious differences, however, was that built into the structure of the church furniture, namely the rood screen: a barrier partially separating the priest and his acolytes in the choir from the congregation. Reminders of this architectural device are to be seen in All Saint's, North Street. York Minster's screen is of stone, and a gateway gives admission into the choir. The celebrating priest would come down to such gates to deliver the bidding prayer for communion.

From surviving wills of the period it is evident that many priests possessed their own breviaries and manuals (often written in a tiny script, easily portable and extremely useful for parish duties). Other books might remain permanently in the church, especially if these were bulky or used solely in church, such as the Mass-book and the Antiphonarium.

The standards of literacy, and Latinity, of the English clergy in general and the York priests in particular were not uniform. The acknowledgement by Church authorities that such problems existed led Bonifacius VIII in his bull *Cum ex eo* of 1298 to allow bishops to grant leave of absence for parish priests to enable them to study at university while still drawing their stipend. What was lacking was a system of basic training for the priesthood. Works such as the *Mammotrectus* (in print by 1470) sought to address this deficiency by guiding priests through the correct pronunciations, and meanings, of words they encountered in biblical and other texts.

A further incongruity of the English Church of 1500 was that not all priests were beneficed: that is, many men in priestly orders had no parish. Such men scraped a living by acting as chantry priests, by singing masses for the souls of the dead or by a little teaching.

Conscientious priests were all too aware of these drawbacks and problems. One of these priests was Robert Avissede, a former chaplain of the little church of S. Gregory between Micklegate and Toft Green.

In the first paragraph of his prologue of 1497, he baldly states:

'However at the present time many are unwilling to listen to or to understand about whom (male), whom (female) or whom (plural) the service has been performed: they have not followed the Ordinal nor do they pay attention to newly constituted feasts.' He quotes psalm 35 and goes on: 'Now we must grieve that in God's house we have been raised up such ignorant and unskilled men, not having the will or the inclination to understand or to perform or to recite (the service) correctly: for in one place and another I have found, and I find, and hear, that men of little awareness, careless, not observing procedure, inattentive, is what we have become, even though it is through the foresaid grace that we have been called to the priesthood.

So it is that through this same grace I have proposed to spell out the serial order of service of day to day recital, tailored to the intelligence of everyone. Beginning in the year of the Lord 1497 and on the 24th day of April I shall first set forth the dominical letters by which Sunday will run from year to year throughout the space of the Great Cycle...'

He then enters, in considerable detail, upon an explanation of this Table (which occupies seven pages). The Table is set out in three columns to the page. Each entry, on its separate line, gives the dominical (or Sunday) letter, in this manner: A for a year in which the first of January falls on a Sunday, G when it falls on Monday, F for Tuesday, E for Wednesday, D for Thursday, C for Friday and B for Saturday.

By each of these dominical letters is placed a number from one to five. This is to distinguish which of the five possible weeks Easter falls in.

So, if Easter falls on any of the dates 22 to 28 March it is allocated the number one, and so on. In tabular form, thus:-

Years beginning on		Easter falling within	
		22-28 March	1
Sun.	A	29 March – 4 April	2
Mon.	G	5-11 April	3
Tues.	F	12-18 April	4
Wed.	E	19-25 April	5
Thurs.	D		
Fri.	C		
Sat.	B		

So Avissede's starting year of 1497 is designated A1 as it begins on Sunday and Easter falls on the 26th March within week 1. The next year, 1498, is G4 : it begins on Monday and Easter is on 15th April within week 4. 1499 is F2 : it begins on Tuesday and Easter comes on the 31st March within week 2.

Leap years, because of the insertion of an extra day in February, follow the patterns of two years. Avissede therefore gives them two letters, as he does for 1500. It began on Wednesday and so it is given the letter of E. From the intercalated day in February for the rest of the year it follows the pattern of D years. This notably affects the date of the feast of S. Matthias: in 1500 his feast would be celebrated on Tuesday 25 February whereas in the common years 1495 and 1579 his feast- day is Tuesday 24 February.

He also allots space to mark the cycles of moon and sun. He accepts a lunar cycle of 19 years, recording the beginnings of lunar cycles in 1501, 1520, 1539, 1558, 1577 and 1596 and of solar cycles, of 28 years' duration, in 1521, 1549, 1577 – noting the coincidence of the two cycles – and 1605, etc. (The printing of roman numerals is sometimes susceptible to error: Hugo Goes' compositor represents 1605 as M.di.xv, and manuscript corrections, including of 'lunar' and 'solar', are made in the Sydney

Sussex copy to the text both of the Prologue and of the Table, presumably by its first owner, Thomas Sanders.)

After these explanations he continues:

'In addition, after the dominical letters mentioned above, with the years of the Lord and the solar cycles and the lunar too interposed, there will follow the little book, the paltry work of my poor abilities, which will be called the Pica. And all variations of feasts, moveable and immoveable, both when and where they are to occur I shall interweave in my notes.'

He then alludes to the special case of the leap year 1736 when the Sunday of Septuagesima coincides with the feast of S. Peter's Chair: for this he has written the unique section D6. He mentions too a large board hanging up in York Minster, in the vestiary, on which he has made notes 'on many and diverse matters'. He is aware that the special case of 1736 has occurred only three times in the past [in 1204, 672 and 140].

After the seven pages of the Table he refers again to its duration:-

'One should note that, unless the Day of the great Judgement has already intervened, this Table will be concluded on a leap year, and the dominical letters C and B, in the year of the Lord 2028... When it reached the end it will begin again, since it will ever endure as long as the world will endure with mankind living on the Earth.

Let us ever give thanks to God.'

(Next come two and a half pages, largely on explanations of terms, and other notes, ending with directions for three days of the Feast of S. Peter – to whom the Minster is dedicated – then

¶Here begins the Pica, that is the Guide for Priests of the Use of York.

The main body of the text follows, from A1 recto to V3 verso: 117 leaves, 234 pages. Its structure is determined by the dominical letters A, G, F, E, D, C and B, and by the weeks within which Easter falls, namely 1, 2, 3, 4 and 5. The headlines guide the reader through the permutations, under A1, A2, A3, A4, A5: then G1 to G5 and so on, ending with B5 on page 250. (The exceptional case of

D6 occupies 1½ pages from O3 recto to O4 recto).

The sections A 1-4, G 1-4, F 1-4, E 1-4, D 1-4, C 1-4 and B 1-4 are all shorter than the fifth part of these sections. This is to save space, since once Ascension, Whitsun and Corpus Christi are passed the long succession of Sundays after Trinity introduces no major variation. So at the end of June, July or August, at the last line of A1, A2, A3, A4, G1, G2, G3, G4 etc. we read 'etc. Everything as is made clear in the final part of the dominical letter A [i.e. the succession of Feast-days, commemorations etc. for the second half of the year is the same for A1, A2, A3, A4, etc. as will be stipulated for A5, etc.]

A picture of the contents may be seen in these brief extracts: square brackets enclose the translator's additions.

¶ Sunday of the feast of the Dedication of the church: memorial of the Apostles [S.Paul and S.Peter] & of the martyrs etc. Find out how the recital is to be of the service of Dedication at the feast of the same in the first dominical letter A [i.e. in A1] through the whole week. [From A3, 2 July].

¶ Thursday of the Lady. At vespers the antiphon Amen amen [dico vobis: quia plorabitis et flebitis vos..] [From A3, 4 May].

¶ Thursday of the octave of Ascension. Memorial of the martyr [Urbanus, pope and martyr: relegated to a memorial by the octave of the Ascension]. Second vespers from the chapter Erunt of S. Augustine, without a responsorium: with a memorial of the octave & of S. Bede [only a local cononisation] with the versicle Magnificavit [eum in conspectu regum..] [From A3, 25 May].

¶ Friday of S.Augustine [not of Hippo but of Canterbury]. Memorial of S.Bede & of Ascension. At vespers this sole antiphon viri galilei [quid admiramini aspicientes] with the psalm of the day [Dominus regnavit, ps.92]. [From A3, 26 May].

E Fifth

¶ Monday [10 Feb.] of S. Scholastica ¶Tuesday of S. William ¶Wed. chapter from fifth Sunday [after Epiphany] Response as for weekday ¶ Thurs. of the Apostles or of a local [saint] ¶ Fri. of S. Valentine [14 Feb.] ¶ Sat. of the Lady. And it is to be concluded with Alleluia ¶ Sun. [16 Feb.] Septuagesima, 14th day [before] the Kalends of March: memorial of the Virgin ¶ Mon. of weekday:

mass from the Sunday [deferred from Sunday because of the coincidence of Septuagesima] or of the Lady ¶ Tues. of S. William ¶ of weekday ¶ Thurs. of the Lady or of a local feast ¶ Fri. of weekday ¶ Sat. of the Chair of S. Peter [22 Feb.] At Vespers no more than memorial of Sunday just as on Sat. as on Sun. ¶ Sun. [23 Feb.] Sexagesima ¶ Mon. of the feast of S. Mathias except in a leap year because then Mon. [is] of a weekday [and is celebrated on 25 Feb]: mass of Sunday or of S. William ¶ Tues of the feast of S. Mathias ¶ Wed. of a weekday ¶ Thurs. of S. William or of a local feast &c. All as is made clear in the Dominical letter D5 but in common years it is to be said thus: ¶Mon. of the feast of S. Mathias as is mentioned before ¶ Tues. of S. William ¶ Wed. of a weekday ¶ Thurs. of a weekday: mass of the Sunday or of a local feast ¶ Fri. of a weekday.

¶ March

¶ Sat. of the Lady: memorial of the saint [Mathias] ¶ Sun. Quinquagesima and the feast [of S. Chad] is to be deferred [because of the coincidence of Quinquagesima] ¶ Mon. [3 Mar.] of S. Chad [whose feast is properly on 2 Mar.] ¶ Tues. of the Lady ¶ Wed. of the Beginning of Fasting [i.e. Ash Wednesday, the start of Lent] ¶ Thurs. Fri. & Sat. of weekdays ¶ Sun. First of Quadragesima, 7th day [before] the Ides of March ¶ Mon. & Tues. of weekdays ¶ Wed. of S. Gregory [12 Mar.] Ember days [Wed. Fri. & Sat. after 1st Sun. in Lent] ¶ Thurs. Fri. & Sat. of weekdays ¶ Sun. second of Quadragesima ¶ Mon. Tues. & Wed. of weekdays ¶ of S Cuthbert [20 Mar.] ¶ Fri. of S. Benedict ¶ Sat. of weekdays ¶ Sun. Third of Quadragesima ¶ Monday of weekday ¶ Tues. of the Feast of the Annunciation of the blessed Mary [25 Mar.] ¶ Wed. and Thurs. of weekdays ¶ Fri. & Saturday of weekdays ¶ Sun. Fourth of Quadragesima ¶ Mon. of weekdays.

¶April

¶Tues. & Thurs. of weekdays [Wed. 2 April is scored through. A handwritten note at the bottom of the page reads
Wed. of the Visitation of the blessed Mary. This correction to the rubric is found throughout both the York copy and the Sidney Sussex copy. This change was approved for the Northern province in 1513, three years after the printing.]
¶Fri. [4th Apr.] of S. Ambrose ¶ Sat. of weekday ¶Sun. Passion Sunday ¶ Mon. Tues. Wed. Thurs. Fri. and Saturday of weekdays ¶ Sun. Palm Sunday [13 April].

At the conclusion of his lengthy and detailed treatise correcting mistakes in the Sarum Ordinale the liturgical scholar Clement Maydeston remarked

'For the man who keeps the foresaid rules in his memory will scarcely be able to go wrong in the divine service.'

This was a counsel of perfection for the ordering of a highly complex system of worship. For allied to the problems of a constantly shifting calendar was a division in the status of feasts. Feasts were either double or simple. Of the double feasts there were four grades: principal, greater, lesser, lower. Of the simple feasts three main categories existed, but these were further subdivided into those which required a choir, or not: a procession, or not: nocturns, or not: etc. The guiding principle was that a lesser feast yielded to a greater: but one can sympathize with priests who made mistakes.

Robert Avissede's compilation of 1497 was used. One of its readers was Thomas Hothyrsall, a vicar choral resident in Bedern, who will have compared the prescriptions laid down by Avissede with the practice of divine service in the Minster, where he, as one of the 36 vicars choral, sang the offices. He found many errors in the guide and, after 'unremitting labour of many years', emended and revised the earlier work, presumably by early 1510. Hothyrsall showed his revision to a canon of York Minster, prebendary of Givendale, Dr. Thomas Hannibal, a man already of some distinction (with an impressive diplomatic career yet to come a decade or so later). Hannibal had studied two years at the famous legal university of Bologna and had later been awarded doctorates in both civil and canon law at Cambridge. He agreed to support the revised version and contributed a somewhat florid preface occupying the first two and a quarter pages. Indeed, his name and titles are the first words known to have been printed in York:

Thome Han[n]ibal legu[m] doctoris ac canonici Ebo[rum].

Both Avissede and Hothyrsall must have been aware of the Directorium Sacerdotum of Clement Maydeston (c.1390-1456) written for the sister Use of Sarum. William Caxton's edition of 1487 was followed by ten other editions by 1508, three printed by Wynkyn de Worde and five by Richard Pynson. The last seven editions, from 1497 onwards, were all revised by William Clerke.

Clerke, like his patron Thomas Rotherham (Archbishop of York 1480 to 1500), had been a Fellow of King's College, Cambridge. He followed Rotherham to York where, some time after April

1492, he married a widow, Alison Doddington. They lived, it seems, in High Petergate, for in her will of 5 July 1509 she directs

'..I will my nebours frome Stanegait ende to Bothome bar be at my Derige [a word introducing part of the funeral service] and at dener..'

Avissede possibly and Hothyrsall probably will have profited from conversations on the Pica with a liturgical scholar of Clerke's experience.

The first liturgical book of the Use of York known to have been printed is the York Breviary of 1 May 1493, during the archbishopric of the highly respected Thomas Rotherham. It is a fine edition, printed in red and black, by the excellent German printer Johann Hamman, whose workshop was in Venice. Of that print-run of perhaps 300 to 400 one copy survives. It was once in the possession of Marmaduke Fothergill (1652-1731), a York man, born in Walmgate. It is to him that York Minster Library owes its possession of the York Pica, printed by Hugo Goes in Stonegate by Monday 18 February 1510.

Was Goes the first printer to live and work in York? In the lengthy list of those admitted in 12 Henry VII (1497) as Freemen of York, and so able to practise their trade, was 'Fridericus Freez', behind whose anglicized name lies the Dutch surname de Vries. He is styled 'bookbynder & stationer'. If he did print, nothing has survived. We should remember the 1493 York Breviary, surviving in only one copy, and the York Pica, in two.

Ephemera, like the broadsheets Autolycus hawked, and books subjected to heavy and frequent use, often perish easily to survive in a mutilated state. But the two greatest factors ensuring the almost complete destruction of England's Catholic service books were firstly the Protestant Reformation and then the Edwardian order of 1549 for their annihilation. Even before 1549 Henry's antipathies towards Catholic practice and veneration resulted in measures which have scarred both our copies, Sidney Sussex and York Minster.

In June 1535[1] the King issued a proclamation commanding the pope's name to be erased out of all prayers1 and Church books: followed in September 1538 by another proclamation for the abolition of counterfeit saints. The cult of S. Thomas was specifically outlawed on 16 November 1538. The unknown owner of the York copy, and Thomas Sanders of the Cambridge copy, both complied. The consequences may be seen throughout the pages of both books in the inking out by Sanders of 'papa' and 'pape' and of Thomas of Canterbury (Thomas Becket), perhaps without enthusiasm, as the offending words are still easily legible. The owner of the York copy has possibly used a sharp pen-knife as the letters have to be guessed.

Two Oxford men of the early 1530s bear the name Thomas Sanders. Our Thomas corrected vigilantly throughout his book, recording his name twice in ownership inscriptions.

Liber thome sanderi cuius deus misereatur
is written in a neat hand at the head of the first page:
Thomas Sander's book on whom may God have mercy.

At V3 verso he also records the price he paid for it: 8d (eight pence). This is no guarantee of the original selling price if it was c.1530 that the book was acquired. But it is not out of line with the prices realised by the Oxford bookseller John Dorne in 1520, whose day-book we possess. A 'Manipulus curatorum' was sold for 8d, the Epistles of Q.Horatius, without commentary, fetched 4d, the Fables of Aesopus 3d, a Terentius, unbound, a shilling, Erasmus' New Testament, bound in leather, 2s. But for a chantry priest, unbeneficed, scraping a living on £5 a year even 8d represented one part in 150 of his annual income.

There is no naming in the Pica of its publisher. The printer, Hugo Goes, who states his name and address at folio 126 recto, may have printed the work as a commercial venture, knowing there was a ready market for the book. Hothyrsall himself will not have been able to afford to lay out the necessary funds. The Dean and Chapter must be considered the likely backer of the publication. If

---

[1] The Processionale ad Usum Sarum of 1517 has 'sacerdos … dicat in lingua materna sic:
    Oremus pro ecclesia Romana et pro papa et archiepiscopis …'
   In the same rubric of the 1544 edition this requirement to pray for the Roman Church and for the pope has been changed to a directive to 'pray for the Anglican Church and for our king…'
    'pro ecclesia Anglicana et pro rege nostro et archiepiscopis…'

so, the decision would largely have rested with the 'quattuor personae', namely James Harrington the Dean (on a huge stipend of over £300 a year): Dr. William Melton the Chancellor, himself a published author: John Perott the Precentor: and Dr. Robert Langton the Treasurer. A third candidate would be Archbishop Christopher Bainbridge, a former Dean of York, recently translated from Durham.

Whoever it was who paid for the printing he or they may well have miscalculated the demand for the Pica, for later in the same year 1510 a dispute arose about the ownership of 570 Picas – among other liturgical books – held in Petergate. It is also worth remembering that the York Breviary paid for and imported by John Gaschet (dated 15 Oct. 1526) included a Pica, as did the York Breviary of 22 Aug. 1533 also imported and published by Gaschet.

The book collates ✠^{8} A-V^6 so 128 leaves are called for. The Sidney Sussex copy is textually complete but lacks the last leaf, presumably blank. The York copy has 115 leaves, lacking F 3-4, G 6, P 3-4, Q 3-4 and the final quire V 1-6. Its dimensions are 190 x 119mm. Each text page has the headline and, usually, 30 lines.

Goes' compositor acquitted himself well enough on the main body of a highly challenging text with its thousands of abbreviations. Mistakes with roman numerals are understandable: the errors in Dr. Hannibal's preface may suggest a rushed job from late, manuscript copy.

But local pride has its place: York and Yorkshire can salute Robert Avissede and Thomas Hothyrsall: the men who backed them: and Goes' team of printers working long hours in February 1510, in Stonegate in the heart of York.

Bibliography to appendix one

- A Biographical Register of the University of Oxford A.D.1501 to 1540: A.B. Emden (Oxford 1974)
- A History of York Minster, ed. G.E. Aylmer and R. Cant: chapter II by Barrie Dobson, chapter V by Claire Cross (Oxford 1977)
- Antiphonarium Romanum (Solesmis 1891)
- Bibliographie der Breviere 1501-1850 von Hanns Bohatta (Stuttgart, Nieuwkoop 1963)
- Breviarium ad Usum Insignis Ecclesie Eboracensis, ed. J.R. Lawley for Surtees Society vol. 71 (1880), vol. 75 (1883) (Durham)
- Breviarium ad Usum Sarum, fasciculus II, ed. F.Procter and C. Wordsworth (Cambridge 1879)
- Day-Book of John Dorne. ed. F. Madan in Collectanea First Series (Oxford 1885)
- Directorium Sacerdotum, Clement Maydeston, ed. W. Cooke and C. Wordsworth (London 1901, 1902)
- Fasti Ecclesiae Anglicanae 1300-1541: VI, Northern Province: John Le Neve. and B. Jones (London 1963)
- Handbook of Dates for Students of English History, ed. C.R. Cheney (London 1961)
- Printing in York – from the 1490s: W.K. and E.M. Sessions (York 1976)
- Processionale ad Usum Sarum, ed. W.G. Henderson (Leeds 1882)
- Testamenta Eboracensia vol. V: ed. James Raine for Surtees Society vol.79 (Durham 1884)
- Tracts of Clement Maydeston, ed. C. Wordsworth (London 1894)

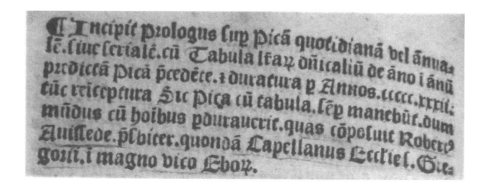

Appendix Two

perhaps John Jackson started the longest continuous line of craftsmen in the north of England at York

John Jackson (1678-1744) served his apprentice with John White, who had been made *Their Majesties Printer for the City of York, and the five Northern Counties.* This award was given to John White by William and Mary, for printing their historic manifesto, shortly before the flight from England of King James II.

In 1703, John Jackson set up on his own account in Grape Lane and printed a book of anthems for Thomas Wandless the Minster organist. In 1704 he was again printing a sermon for the Minster. It was a thirty-two-page thanksgiving sermon, printed shortly after the occasion of the Battle of Blenheim. He was born in 1678 in the parish of St Michael le Belfry. He married Mary, they had two children William 1702 and Thomas 1703. John remarried and had a further five children Elizabeth 1705, John 1707, Rachel 1710, Christopher 1711 and Thomas 1712.

His son John Jackson (1707-1771) married Magdalene Conyer in 1739. He was made a freeman of the city in 1733 and in 1741 started the York Gazetteer, a publication with which Laurence Sterne was associated. Laurence Sterne's book Tristram Shandy was later printed in York in 1760. There is no imprint. We know that Sterne was well acquainted with Jackson. It would be quite natural to have the book printed here at Jackson House. If so, we printed the first modern novel. John Jackson printed for James Ray of Whitehaven the complete history of the Rebellion.

Francis Jackson succeeded to his father's business in 1771 and continued to run it until 1790. It was not a reflection of his work that he ended up in Allen's charity.

The Jacksons' office at 53 Petergate and 7 Grape Lane has continued to this day as a printing house. Commencing certainly by 1703, it is believed to be the longest continuous line of craftsmen printers in York and possibly the North of England.

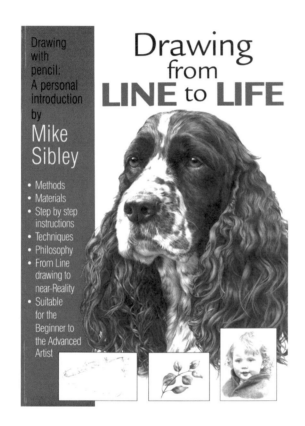

After the Jacksons the printing house was continued in the early part of the nineteenth century, by William Storry and his son, William Francis Storry. It was later taken over by W. T. Wickeley and then B. Wickeley until 1835. William Sotheran, grandson of the bookseller at the sign of the bible in Stonegate subsequently became a printer. York's castle museum is in possession of three guard books of specimens of William Sotheran's printing stating quantities supplied with dates ranging from 1837-1886. There are also extant ledgers at Jackson House listing each job he produced. He printed for the Minster, the Yorkshire Philosophical Society and the York Hospital amongst many others.

Towards the end of the nineteenth century, Sotheran sold the business to his apprentice Valentine Morley. His two sons, Henry –a freeman of the city- and Walter continued after Valentine's death. They also ran a post office, stationers, newsagents and lending library.

The name of the firm had become H. Morley & Sons, before the death of Henry Morley in 1910, at which time the succession passed to Frank Morley, who was also a freeman of the city by patrimony.

Upon the death of Frank in 1932, twin Morley Sons of the fourth generation, Frank Leslie and George Eric, took control and formed H. Morley and Sons ltd. Both brothers were away on war service between 1939-1945, and during this period, Leslie's wife Annie Lavinia, continued the printing business in a most able and effective manner.

In the mid-1960s, John Wheater took over the running of the company. By January 1983 Michael Sessions had moved his office to Jackson House from Huntington Road. His father Bill Sessions had bought the business in 1972 largely for historic reasons.

During the 1980s Jackson House became a centre for producing antiquarian book catalogues for booksellers all over the country and even in Europe. This led to the Waddleton Chronology printed and published by Quacks for Cambridge University and the Heath Trilogy, recording the engravings of James Heath A.R.A and Charles and his two sons Frederick and Alfred 1779-1878.

The acquisition of the Radius regional area directory publications from Ray Howden in 2000 increased the proportion of published printed work.

On the 18th February 2010 the staff consisted of the Manager Horst Siegfried Meyer I.T., Mandy O'Sullivan, Richard Cousans, Laura Anderson, Hillary Bibby, and the board, emeritus president Bill Sessions, chairman Michael Sessions, company secretary and director, Horst Meyer, E Sue Sessions, and Timothy Jonathan Sessions.

The company name changed in 1986 to Soabar Sessions ltd when it was demerged from William Sessions Ltd, the other Sessions family printing company thus making it completely separate and in effect in competition. In 2010 William Sessions Ltd went into administration, leaving Soabar Sessions

Ltd trading as Quacks as the only Sessions family run York printing and publishing company.

In 2017 the printing and publishing concern at Jackson House came under the ownership of Radius Publishing Ltd which continues the publishing of the Radius and the imprint Quacks Books. Martin Nelson was appointed the Managing Director with Michael Sessions Chairman with Lesley Seeger the creative director. Katy Midgley, the granddaughter of Ray Howden, from whom the Radius publications were acquired, was the head of the design team until the birth of her daughter in 2021. Today, Rachel Hopkins is in the design team, we have a digital team, and Jackie is in administration.

Around 75% of the Jackson House activity revolves around the Radius. However as Dickens once said. *Expenditure £1.01 income £1.00 brings gloom and the other way round brings happiness.* Similarly at Quacks the book printing and publishing and other printing that makes up 25% of our activity is very important and equally enjoyable.

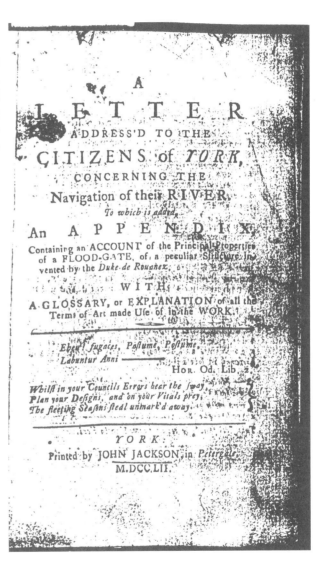

A
LETTER
ADDRESS'D TO THE
CITIZENS of *YORK*,
CONCERNING THE
Navigation of their RIVER.
To which is added,
An APPENDIX,
Containing an ACCOUNT of the Principal Properties of a FLOOD-GATE, of a peculiar Structure Invented by the *Duke de Roueñez*;
WITH
A GLOSSARY, or EXPLANATION of all the Terms of Art made Use of in the WORK.

Eheu! fugaces, Poſtume, Poſtume, Labuntur Anni — Hor. Od. Lib. 2.

Whilſt in your Councils Errors bear the ſway, Plan your Deſigns, and on your Vitals preys, The fleeting Seaſons ſteal unmark'd away.

YORK:
Printed by JOHN JACKSON, in *Petergate.*
M.DCC.LII.

Yearsley Village to York

The River Foss

— Its History and Natural History

by

Michael Fife and Peter Walls

ROMAN ANCHORAGE : ROYAL FISHPOND
MEDIEVAL MOAT : MODERN FOOTPATH

Footpath Maps and Suggested Walks
on pages 64 to 67.

BADGERS
of Yorkshire
& Humberside

R.J.PAGET
A.L.V.MIDDLETON

Appendix Three

the Sessions Book Trust – the first fifty-five years
1967-2022

reg charity number 529735

In memory of the Co-Founders of the Sessions Book Trust William Kaye Sessions (1915 – 2013) and Anne King (née Sessions) (1919 – 2013), their Founding Trustee Ethelwyn Margaret Sessions (née Lidbetter) (1912 – 1994), and Patrick Irvine King (1922 – 2007).

John P S King MA (Oxon), 2023.

The Sessions Book Trust came into being with the Trust Deed of 26 July 1967 between the Founders William Kaye Sessions of 6 Rawcliffe Grove, York and his sister Edith Anne King (née Sessions) of 55 York Road, Northampton, and the first Trustees being the two Founders and E Margaret Sessions, the wife of William Kaye Sessions.

The Trust Deed begins with a description of the inspiration of Mary Sessions, the widow of William Sessions, the Founders' grandfather:

'Mary Sessions, a widow with young children to support yet with slender means, was well known for her charity. The giver went with gifts and her visits amongst the poor caused her to be known as the angel of Walmgate; Walmgate being then a slum area. The example set by Mary Sessions and by other members of the Sessions family encourages the Founders to think that if they give their knowledge of printing, publishing and publicity, together with such sums as they can afford, they may be able to render some small service to the Community. The Founders believe that there are many ideas of inherent value to the community which are not sufficiently well known, owing to lack of publication. They have therefore resolved to constitute a trust, to be known as "The Sessions Trust".

This was the original name of the Trust, which was later amended to "The Sessions Book Trust". It had an initial capital of £2 to which £4,000 was added, all of which was originally invested in William Sessions Ltd, The Ebor Press.

The inaugural meeting of the Sessions Trust was held on 21 October 1967 and at the next meeting on 11 February 1968 three projects were discussed: the re-printing of 'The Quakers – Their Story and Message' by A. Neave Brayshaw; the publishing and printing of a 32 page booklet on 'The Strays and Ways of York' for the York Group; and a 120 page book of historical essays to mark the 19th centenary in 1971 of the coming of the Roman 9th Legion to York, for the Royal Commission on Historical Monuments.

Anne King's husband Patrick I King was invited to join the Sessions Book Trust's meetings from 15 June 1969. They both attended and contributed to every meeting until 2006. They brought their individual talents as historians to bear on the wide range of projects and scripts which were originated by other Trustees or came to the Trust's attention over the years.

From the beginning the range and scope of the publications which the Sessions Book Trust has supported by grants showed great variety. Naturally there was a wide range of books on Quaker beliefs, history and personages, but in addition publications on York and its history, as well as features of its natural history. The Trust supported the publication of works on travel, local history, poetry, memoirs, meditations, the history of printing in the UK and Ireland, industry, commerce, war and peace.

The Minutes of the Trust's Meeting of 20 November 1971 note that 11,125 books had been produced since the Trust began its work, including 'The Strays and Ways of York' (1968 and 1970), 'Roman York' (1970 and 1971), 'Skelton Village' (1971), 'Yorkshire Flooding' (1971), 'Tukes of York' (1971).

Over the years several Quaker and other charitable trusts made grants to the Sessions Book Trust to support its work in religious, educational and natural historical printing and publishing. These bodies include the Joseph Rowntree Foundation, the Joseph Rowntree Reform Trust, the Marsden Charitable Trust, the Oliver Sheldon Trust, the W A Cadbury Trust, the Bournville Charitable Trust, among others.

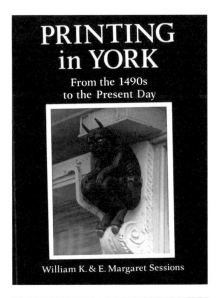

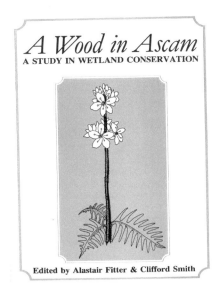

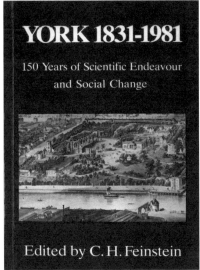

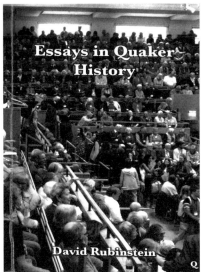

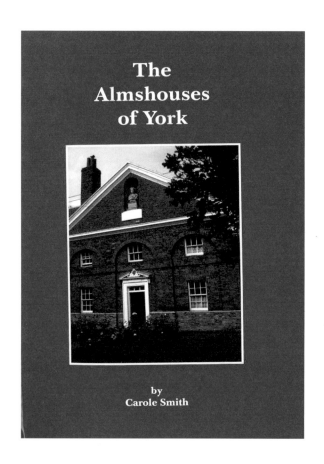

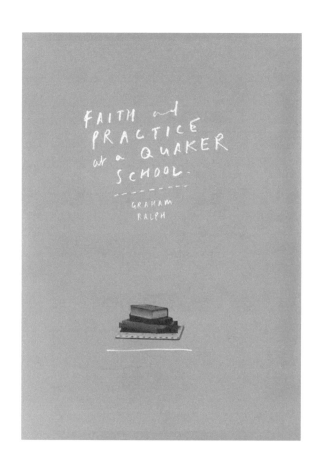

'The River Foss' (1973) 'Badgers of Yorkshire & Humberside' (1974), 'Printing in York' (1976) 'A Wood in Ascam' (1979), 'York 1831-1981' (1981), 'Energy Unbound' (1981), continued the trend of Natural History books, York and Quaker titles.

By the end of the 20th century the Sessions Book Trust's support for a wide range of publications had enlarged significantly to include the following titles from 1997 – 2000:

'Quakers and the American Revolution' (Arthur Mekeel), 'York's Blue Coat & Grey Coat Schools', 'Indian Tapestry: Some Quaker Threads in the History of India, Pakistan and Bangladesh' (Marjorie Sykes with addition by Geoffrey Carnall), 'The Sufferings of Early Quakers' (Joseph Besse), 'Directory of York Gold & Silversmiths' (Hugh Murray), 'Women and Quakerism' (Christine Trevett), 'John Woolman' (David Sox), 'The Foss Navigation and the Effect on its Hinterland' (Tessa Mitchell), 'James Nayler': 'Clouded Quaker Star' (Vera Massey), 'Pacifists in Action' (Deryck Moore), 'Non-Violent Responses' (ed. John Lampen), 'New Earswick Nature Reserve: the first half century (W K Sessions)', 'Quakers and the Arts' (David Sox), among many more.

Since the millennium 'Blessed City: Biography of Edward Bairstow' (Francis Jackson) first edition 1996, revised 1997 reprinted 2003, 'The Biographical Dictionary of British Quakers in Commerce and Industry' (Ted Milligan) 2007, 'The York Almshouses' (Carole Smith) 2010, 'Faith & Practice at a Quaker School,' (Graham Ralph) 2013 reprint 2022, 'Essays in Quaker History' (David Rubinstein) 2016, 'Assisted Dying,' (Barbara Henderson) 2016, 'Reassuring 18th Century Protestants,' (Arthur Holroyd) 2017, 'Great Lives' (Elaine Phillips & Michael Sessions) 2018, 'a History of the Myers & Burnell Cup' (Paul Thorpe) 2019 and reprint 2021,'Passions & Partings', (Jane Mace) 2020, 'Friends and Comrades, How Quakers helped Russians to survive famine and epidemic' (Sergei Nikitin translated by Suzanne Eades Roberts) 2022.

The story of the Sessions Book Trust is one of enormous energy and enthusiasm in finding, bringing into print and publishing a wide range of books, booklets, and pamphlets on Quaker history, as well as on the wider history and natural history of York and its surroundings, and wider international and universal themes. The Trust's publications seek to spread knowledge, insights, thought and practical examples to the community in line with its original stated objectives.

The Trustees' work was supported by the dedication of Mr A. F. Scalway, who was appointed to keep the Trust's accounts and submit its annual Balance Sheet and Statement of Income and Expenditure to the Trustees every year. His role was taken over by Horst Meyer who was also appointed Trustee and Hon. Secretary to the Trust from 1987. From 1994 D. W. Mottram and N. Claxton kept the Trust's Accounts and prepared its Financial Statements.

Over the years several additional members of the Sessions and King families served and serve as Trustees with the Sessions Book Trust, including W Mark Sessions, son of William K Sessions the Co-Founder, and Patricia J Sessions, Mark's wife; Michael H Sessions, also son of William K Sessions, and his wife Lesley C Seeger; Sallie M Dearnley, daughter of William K Sessions; Timothy J Sessions, son of Michael H Sessions; Elizabeth P A Stoner (née King), daughter of Anne King (née Sessions) the Co-Founder; Alison Creed (née King), also daughter of Anne King; Patrick J S King, son of John P S King; John P S King, son of Anne King; and Martin L Nelson.

Today the Sessions Book Trust continues to seek out and bring to publication an increasingly wide variety of books and booklets on educational, artistic, spiritual, philosophical, environmental, historical, and charitable subjects with a view to stimulating and enriching community life based on fundamental Quaker principles of tolerance, respect, compassion, and practical work for the good of all.

Contact details: The Sessions Book Trust, Jackson House, 7 Grape Lane, Petergate, York Yo1 7hu. Email mistyle@quacks.info

The current trustees are Michael Sessions (chairman), Sallie Dearnley, John King, Lesley Seeger, Tim Sessions and Martin Nelson.

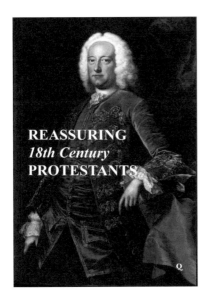

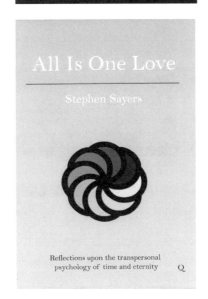

Appendix Four

Which is the most readable Typeface?

Most books are set in the Baskerville typeface. A readable face like Baskerville has serifs and shading (each letter is made up of thick and thin strokes). We read phrases sometimes whole sentences not individual letters. We have become familiar with the unique shapes formed by the twenty six letters of our alphabet lower case letters with their serifs and shading that we have known since we learnt to read. Any deviation from these unique patterns will slow down our reading.

To change your Microsoft Outlook default email typeface from Calibri 11pt to Baskerville 12pt or 14pt go to File > Options > Mail > Stationery and Fonts...select Baskerville... select the options that you want to apply to the default font, such as font style (roman or regular) and font size (12pt or 14pt} ... select this for 'new messages' and for 'replying and forwarding messages' ... select OK all the way back out to save your changes.

To change your default Word typeface from Calibri 11pt to Baskerville 12pt, press and hold Ctrl and D simultaneously to open the Font dialog box or go to Home > Look at the Font Section > Click the small arrow at the bottom right of this section. Select the font and size you want to use, select Default in right hand bottom corner, and then select OK. Select OK.

In 1989 Bill Gates asked the following question, 'Why do we need more fonts?. We've got a serif, a sans, and a monospace font. Why do we need more?'...

In 1999 Microsoft added a further 100 typefaces to their software collection. Most of these are without serifs or shading, and therefore will slow your reading as does Calibri and Arial and all sans serif faces due to their lack of the familiar shading and serifs. In 2007 they changed their default typeface from Times New Roman a shaded serif typeface to Calibri as according to Microsoft, "Typefaces go in and out of fashion." In 2021 Microsoft requested new designs for their default typeface. It had to be in the "grotesque sans serif" genre, a style defined by block-style letters without calligraphic flourish or contrast between thick and thin strokes. The position of Head of Typeface Design at Microsoft should not exist as our so familiar alphabet and its so familiar typeface Baskerville go together like a horse and carriage and cannot be tampered with. Microsoft would not dream of changing the letters of the alphabet so why change the way these letters have been shown to us since our births. Baskerville remains the most readable Microsoft typeface and always will do. The publishing world is not wrong, Microsoft is.

The Baskerville Typeface

Baskerville is a serif typeface designed with shaded letters in the 1750s by John Baskerville (1706–1775) in Birmingham, England, and cut into metal by punchcutter John Handy. Baskerville is the most read book typeface. It was intended as a refinement of what are now called old-style typefaces (gothic).

Compared to earlier designs popular in Britain, Baskerville increased the contrast between thick and thin strokes, making the serifs sharper and more tapered, and shifted the axis of rounded letters to a more vertical position. The curved strokes are more circular in shape, and the characters became more regular. These changes created a greater consistency in size and form, influenced by the calligraphy Baskerville had learned and taught as a young man. Baskerville's typefaces remain the most used typeface in books and therefore ebooks due to their familiarity and readability.

In the twentieth century the Fry Foundry of Bristol made their version of Baskerville, probably cut by their typefounder Isaac Moore. Marketed in the twentieth century as "Fry's Baskerville" or "Baskerville Old Face", a digitisation of this typeface is included with all Microsoft software.

Francis Jackson, a contemporary of John Baskerville has been praised favourably for the similarity in his poster design to Baskerville. The Frys Foundry was owned by Quakers. It is a book face with longer ascenders and descenders which aids readability further than the truncated ascenders and descenders of the newspaper face Times New Roman.

Tenorite	**Tenorite Display**
Bierstadt	**Bierstadt Display**
Skeena	**Skeena Display**
Seaford	Seaford Display
Grandview	Grandview Display

Appendix Five

The Quincentenary of Book Printing in York by the Yorkshire Post Journalist John Woodcock

Standfirst: At a time when some are writing it off, York is celebrating the printed word. Five centuries ago the first book in the North came off the press, and 250 years later the first novel. John Woodcock reports, Mike Gowling also of the Yorkshire Post took the photos of Keith Walls reading the Pica.

Just after Christmas 2009 a headline asked 'Have books turned their last page?' It was in response to record sales of electronic versions of the written word.

Obituaries for the hardcover and paperback are appearing thick and fast and seem a little less absurd when they coincide with the passing of a bookshop chain whose collapse was in part due to competition from the internet.

Virtual libraries are beginning to replace bookshelves, and Amazon.com has experienced its first day when e-books outsold the physical version.

York knows about revolutions involving words and how they're read. Last time around it was at the forefront of change, which makes the closure of its branch of Borders particularly ill-timed. Behind the doomed bookseller's empty store the city is about to celebrate 500 years of printing and paper-made books, and how they helped shape the nation's history.

In and around Stonegate, its most famous thoroughfare, ink-stained craftsmen were among the first with the means to spread the word on behalf of monarchs, politicians, the church, rebels, visionaries, gossips, and traders advertising their dubious potions and 'female pills'.

February 18, 1510, was a bad day for York's scribes and their quills. They confronted a technological challenge as profound as that facing today's High Street retailers from online rivals; one as daunting as the battle being waged by the pages of a Penguin Classic, with their crinkly feel and papery smell, against a pocket size e-reader screen.

In what was then called Steengate, an immigrant from Antwerp called Hugo Goes followed William Caxton's lead and produced a book on a wooden press with individual metal letters and movable type. The *Directorium Sacerdotum* was a bestseller among the clergy because it was an extensive ecclesiastical calendar - 234 white pages in black letter Latin text informing them when services should be held in line with the changing dates of Easter.

It was the first recorded book printed north of Oxford and only two copies survive, one of them in York Minster Library. It's about the size of a modern paperback, has since been bound in calf, and is dwarfed by many of the ancient tomes in the cathedral's collection. In this case size is misleading. The compact *Pica*, Latin for magpie and given the name because printing then meant black and white, helped establish York as a major publishing centre, with all the benefits, upheavals and dangers which accompanied communication via the printed word.

There was the 16th century equivalent of China's censorship of Google. Provincial printing was severely restricted, breaches were a penal offence and Wardens of the Worshipful Company of Stationers were empowered to search for prohibited and unlicensed books outside London. York survived the purges and in 1642, in the build-up to the Civil War, Charles I based the King's Printer in the city. In the quadrangle of St. William's College the timbers and metal pieces of the Royal Press were kept busy producing His Majesty's responses to the declarations of Parliament.

Nearly 50 years later another printer in York was at the heart of new intrigue surrounding the throne. John White had a workshop in Coffee Yard, off Stonegate, and was known to the advisers of William of Orange who'd landed with an army in Devon in response to invitations from Protestants to challenge the Catholic reign of James II.

White risked everything to print William's manifesto and appeared to have backed a loser when he was jailed in Hull, awaiting torture and execution, before James fled to France. King William and Queen Mary expressed their gratitude by appointing White "Their Majesties' Printer for the City of York and the five Northern Counties'.

After his death his widow Grace earned her place in history too by launching the city's first newspaper, the *York Mercury*. It soon led to more public sheets and a contributor who, in the narrow lanes and alleyways awash with printers' ink, wrote himself into literary immortality.

One of White's apprentices was John Jackson who in 1703 opened a print shop in Grape Lane where the craft is still practised today. From there Jackson's son published the *York Gazetteer* and carried political articles from a young country vicar, Laurence Sterne. For his pains Jackson was physically attacked by a Tory supporter who also threatened the clergyman. In the event the Reverend Sterne's writing gifts lay elsewhere and in 1760, at his own expense, he had published and printed in the city the first two slim volumes of *The Life and Opinions of Tristram Shandy, Gentleman*.

He offered subsequent sections to the London publisher who initially had rejected the work. In a letter to him Sterne wrote: 'The book shall be printed here and the impression sent up to you for as I live in York, and shall correct every proof myself, it shall go perfect into the world, and be printed in so creditable a way as to paper, type, &c., as to do no dishonour to you......'

Tristram Shandy is now considered a masterpiece, and often regarded as the first 'modern' novel. In the words of JB Priestley: 'Modern literature begins with Sterne'.

In which case the printing of modern literature began in York, claims Michael Sessions. He's the fourth generation of his family to print there and his oak-beamed premises in Grape Lane reflect how the industry has evolved. He uses computerised technology for today's customers but in another part of Jackson House there's a bibliographic workshop which pays tribute to his predecessors: iron presses, the metal version of typefaces such as 8pt Gloucester, 10pt Old Style Bold, 24pt Samson Script and 36pt Garamond, and how printing terms such as 'out of sorts, 'dab hand' and 'ps and qs' entered our everyday language.

Sessions has been largely responsible for the York exhibition celebrating book printing in the region. And with a sub-title that advances the story from 1510 to 2510 he scoffs at the doubters in his confidence that the printed word will be around for least the next 500 years.

"For all the impact of computers, more paper is being used now than ever before," he points out, "and in one form or another printing will remain a fundamental of life. Caxton's revolution had a massive impact on society and what he introduced continues to develop. Electronic technology is not making print redundant but taking it to exciting new levels."

In the Minster Library they also know about the perils of the printer's art. They have a copy of the Wicked Bible, so-called because in 1631 a compositor typesetting the Ten Commandments forgot, by accident or mischief, to add a word of three letters. The seventh Commandment read: 'Thou shalt commit adultery'.

* The exhibition is being held in Grays Court, Chapter House Street (near the Minster) 14-18 February, 2010 11am-4pm. It includes demonstrations of a historic printing press. For information info@quacks.info or 01904 635967

Suggested sidebar:

Latest figures reveal the extent of the threat to printed books from electronic alternatives. Last year two billion books were sold in the United States but the figure was down nearly five percent on 2008 and is expected to fall another two percent this year.

Waterstone's, now the only UK-wide specialist bookseller since the collapse of Borders, saw sales decline by 8.5pc over the Christmas period.

Meanwhile in the US sales of e-books are soaring and will be worth an estimated billion dollars by 2012 as new products emerge from tech companies like Apple. At the same time Google is intent on scanning and posting every book ever written.

But Print Yorkshire, which promotes the fifth largest employer in the region, is optimistic. Having inspired a revolution in communications and education in Caxton's day, it says the industry is now a major player in the digital age.

Paper-based printing still accounts for most of the industry's output and new technology is improving its quality. New media is reliant on print in many ways – e-readers for example, provide electronic versions of books that have already been printed.

Print Yorkshire recently won funding for projects to explore technology that would enable electronic circuits to be printed onto paper or plastic. That would create another revolution with endless possibilities. Eventually it could lead to gadgets like a mobile phone being printed on a box of corn flakes.

Michael Sessions gives the up-to-date figures for books sold in 2021:

The number of books sold in the United Kingdom reached more than 212 million in 2021, increasing year by year since 2012. Printed books continue to outsell ebooks four to one and both have been increasing by over 20% in recent years. The York Press has just reported that the largest bookshop in York, Lucius Books, is about to open in Micklegate, in 2024.

Appendix Six

Quincentenary luncheon:

introductory remarks by Michael Sessions to the guests.

Welcome to the 18th February 2010 quincentenary luncheon. We are also celebrating a millennium of print for York and Yorkshire. That is we have had 500 years of book printing and there will be at least another 500 years of innovative printing before we reach our millennium. The future is bright.

I would like to put on record my thanks to Nicholas Rogers archivist of Sidney Sussex College Library for his admirable suggestion that brought the only substantially complete copy of the Pica back to York for this celebration. What an honour it is to have him with us today. For those that do not know him he will be sitting next to my Father this lunch time.

Nicholas made very few conditions over the lending of this valuable book. However one of them was that it should be loaned to a Trust not a company.

21 years ago as Philip Chapman and I were walking Through the Vikos Gorge in the Pindus Mountains in north west Greece I turned to Philip and said do you really think it is necessary to set up a charity to honour this fine line of craftsmen printers that Quacks has inherited. His definitive answer, unusual for a solicitor was, yes. If his answer had been no the Pica might not be with us today. The John Jackson Trust is the charity that loaned the Pica for 5 days from Sidney Sussex College Cambridge.

Other people we should be grateful to in no particular order are:- Hugones Goes (pronounce Goose) for printing the Pica in Steengate 500 years ago. Robert Barker for carrying on this line of craftsmen printers and becoming the first of 2 York Kings Printers in 1642, and John White the second Kings Printer who was Quacks founding craftsman John Jackson's boss.

More about that on the Inky Walk at 3pm. Meet in Grays Court when Ray Alexander will take you on a short walk which will probably last around an hour.

We should thank Thomas Wanless the editor of the Anthems for York Minster printed by John Jackson his oldest extant book printed in 1703. Interesting enough although Thomas is not here the link with the Minster continues. David Potter the master bell ringer produced only last December the definitive book on bell ringing at York Minster and around York. It has been a pleasure to produce this sumptious book and thank you David and Christine for being here today. I would like to include with David and Christine Potter, Keith Walls author of a history of the Franciscan monk, John Bromyard. Keith is a railwayman's son brought up in the East Riding and enjoyed times on farms near Ripon and Cumberland. An Athlete at school in Pocklington he won three under 19 Yorkshire discus titles. Later he worked for the Forestry Commission, as a freelance journalist. Over the last ten years he has developed interests in the Dominican Order, late medieval history and filming in York with Geoff Kelly. Ann Holt and her husband David Rubinstein author of The Yorkshire Philosophical Society a social history 1822-2000, Norman Scooter author of the Crystal Gazers, Graham Best, compiler of Songs of Dead Laughter (the poetry of Gertrude Bell), Peter Miller of Spelmans book seller and compiler of catalogues and organising with help from others the York National Book Fair, the largest regional book fair in the country, Philip Chapman already mentioned of Mitchells solicitors, David Hyam of Ware and Kay solicitors and Rachel Alexander-Hill, Terry Casey of the Insurance Partnership and Ann his wife, and Lesley Seeger colourist who are all hear today and have graced Jackson House as our customers. Thank you for keeping us in business.

Today we meet in the Jacques Sterne room of Grays Court.

How lucky we are to be able to use this room of Helen Heraty's house. I would like to thank Helen for allowing us to use her lower gallery for the exhibition and this room for lunch. Jaques Sterne, Precentor of York Minster, built this extension and lived here in the 1740s. He with his Whig background backed the York Gazetteer printed by John Jackson and would have been in constant touch with the editor his nephew Laurence Sterne, The author of the first modern novel, according to J. B. Priestley printed just over 250 years ago here in York.

Also here today are a cousin of Keith Walls, Margaret Grandidge and her husband Reginald. Keith has been a constant source of support since last September when this idea was first muted. I am extremely grateful to him. Keith has also brought Gerry Webb and Judy his wife. Jerry was curator of Fairfax

House for many years. Of course Keith is a many talented man. He reads latin. He also has thrown the discus rather well for Yorkshire. It is not surprising that he has brought another athlete along, Geoff Kelly, film maker, local historian, but above all a long jumper, amongst other sporting activities. Whilst mentioning sporting activity Terry Casey was a fine shot putter at the same school.

Well who have I not mentioned. Have we any librarians, readers, academics, printers or trustees of the John Jackson Trust that I have not already listed. I am glad to say we have. Professor Emeritus Graham Parry will give the vote of thanks on behalf of the guests. One of his interest areas is Laurence Sterne. Dr Phil Quinlan, a fine tennis player and Dr Amanda Sowden represent the current staff of York University and in particular the growing interest of the John Jackson Trust in the Psychology of readability. Bernard and Mary Barr and Gillian and Roger Holmes represent the Minster Library and the City Library, whilst Stephanie Hanson apart from being a good friend of Lesley's as are Gillian and Roger Holmes really enjoys reading books.

Finally to the Printers Phil Achurch, Robert Gallagher, Brian Colton, Horst Meyer, Penny and Robert Kealey Myself and Lesley, and my Father. Phil Achurch, an engineer, now managing Director of Soabar. Soabar specialise in sending information to the point of need through their satellites in Dalian, China, Istanbul, Turkey or Leicester. Robert Gallagher is Soabar's Production Director. I am especially pleased to have Brian Colton here as amongst other things he started his working life as a compositor (read my several references to the lost art and discipline of the compositor in the style book.) Brian has worked on the sales side of both Soabar and Quacks. His son flies him to places like Hawaii at the drop of a hat.

Horst Meyer director and manager of Quacks and the company secretary and a trustee of the John Jackson Trust. a great colleague and friend. His tennis is improving too. Brian Jardine, his tennis forehand is masterly and unique, a trustee of the John Jackson Trust. He works for a slightly larger Trust started by another Quaker, Joseph Rowntree.

Myself, I am currently Chairman of Soabar and Chairman of Quacks and trustee of the John Jackson Trust. Lesley Seeger*, my girl friend, art therapist at York's NHS hospital, printmaker and artist, and last but by no means least my Father, Bill Sessions, 94 not out, as he sometimes says.

Is he a printer, yes, an author, yes, a publisher, yes, a dad, yes, also a grandfather 10 times over and a great grand father too. Robert Davies the author of a Memoire of the York Press listed the extant books printed in York in the 18th century. Mum and Dad used this as a basis for their book Printing in York brought out for the Caxton Quincentenary in 1976. They had learnt that Morleys had this fine line of Craftsmen back to 1703. The company was acquired in 1972.

And that is largely why I am standing here today welcoming you all to this celebration. So a thank you to all for coming. Thank you for what you represent and enjoy this celebration. The future of print is bright.

*Michael married Lesley on the 12th May 2012.

bibliography

Nicholas Barker, *the York Gospels,* 1986, Roxburghe Club, London.

Robert Davies, *a Memoir of the York Press,* a list of the names of sixteenth, seventeenth- and eighteenth-century **York printers** and their extant work in 1868. Reprinted by Spelmans, Mickelgate, York with a new foreword by Bernard Barr in 1975.

Albert Garrett, *a history of Wood Engraving,* 1978 and 1986, Bloomsbury Books, isbn 0 906223 29 6.

John Heath, *the Heath Family Engravers, 17779-1878,* Volume 1, James Heath A.R.A 1757-1834, 1993, Scolar Press, Volume 2 Charles Heath 1785-1848, Frederick Heath, Alfred Heath 1812-96, 1993, Scolar Press; Supplement, Volume 3,1993, Quacks Books, York isbn 0 948333 87 1; John Heath's Catalogue of illustrated Books and prints engraved by the Heath Family 1779- 1878 printed by Quacks the Printer, York.

Marshall McLuhan, *the Gutenberg Galaxy,* the making of typographic man, Routledge and Kegan Paul, 1962.

Douglas C. McMurtrie, *The book, the story of printing and book making,* 1943, Bracken Books, London isbn 85170 326 8.

L.T. Owens, *J. H. Mason 1875-1951 Scholar Printer,* 1976, Frederick Muller, London isbn 0 584 10353 0.

Domenico Porzio, *Lithography, 200 years of art, history and technique,* 1983, Harry Abrams, New York.

Ian Campbell Ross, *Laurence Sterne a life,* 2001, Oxford University Press, isbn o 19 280406 5.

Michael H. Sessions, E. Susan Sessions, William K. Sessions, *from 1704 John Jackson I and II & Francis Jackson printers of Grape Lane and Petergate, York England fl1704-1790,* 2004, Quacks Books, York.

William K. Sessions, *the Kings Printer at York 1642,* 1981, the Ebor Press, York; a Printer's Dozen,1983, the Ebor Press, York; Printing in York with **E. Margaret Sessions,** 1976, Wm. Sessions ltd, York isbn 0 900657 37 5.

Alberic Stackpoole, *The Noble City of York Chapter on Printing in York by W. K. Sessions and E Margaret Sessions,* 1972, Cerialis Press, York.

Hugh Williamson, *Methods of Book Design, The Practice of an Industrial Craft,* 1956, Oxford.

index

Phil Achurch	66
Rachel Alexander-Hill	66
William Alexander	reverse flap
Laura Anderson	viii,48
Robert Avissede	34,36,40,42
Christopher Bainbridge	42
Robert Barker	4
Bernard Barr	ix,66
Mary Barr	66
John Baskerville	5,24,32,58,59
Oliver Beckerlegge	viii
Max Beckmann	viii
Joseph Besse	55
Getrude Bell	66
Graham Best	66
Hilary Bibby	48
Bonifacius VIII	34
Georges Braque	vii,xvii
A.Neave Brayshaw	52
John Bromyard	viii,66
Dr John Burton	5
Geoffrey Carnall	55
Terry & Ann Cassey	66
William Caxton	4,11,24,31,63
Marc Chagall	vi,viii,xvii
Philip A. Chapman	66
Charles I	4,61
Winston Churchill	22
Brian Colton	66
Richard Cousans	viii,48
Jackie Coverdale	xviii,48
Matt Clark	xi
N. Claxton	56
Alison Creed	56
Robert Davies	6,25,66
Sallie Dearnley	56
Maurice Denis	viii
Charles Dickens	x,49
Dr Francis Drake	5
Max Ernst	viii,xvii
Marmaduke Fothergill	41
Fridericus Freez (de Vries)	41
Robert Gallagher	66
John Gaschet	42
John Garbutt	6,30
Hugo Goes	4,24,41,42,60
Mike Gowling	60
Margaret Grandidge	66
Johannes Gutenburg	11,19,20,31
Johann Hamman	41
John Handy	58
Dr Thomas Hannibal	40
James Harrington	42
David Hyam	66
James Heath Charles, Frederick and Alfred	48
John Heath	vi
Eric Heckel	vii
Barbara Henderson	55
Helen Heraty	66
Gillian &Roger Holmes	66
Arthur Holroyd	55
Ann Holt	66
Rachel Hopkins	xviii,48
Thomas Hothyrsall	40,42
Stephen House	66
Ray & Mary Howden	48
Francis Jackson	30,32,45,59

Dr Francis Jackson 55
John Jackson I (senior) vii,5,29,30,32,45,48,66
John Jackson II xvii,6,30,32,45
James II 4,24,32,45,62
James the Deacon 1
Brian Jardine 66
Geoff Kelly 66
Annabel Kidston vi
Edith Anne King 51,52,56
John Patrick Sessions King xi,56
Patrick John Sessions King 56
Patrick Irvine King 51,52
Karl Klic 12
John Lampen 55
Dr Robert Langton 42
Lanston 12
Andrew Leathley viii,48
Fernand Leger viii
John Locke 29
Loius XIV 29
Robert McClements ix
Marshall McLuhan vii,15
Kauffer E. McNight viii
Jane Mace 55
Guy Malet vii
Marini Marino viii
Duke of Marlborough (John Churchill) 4
Margaret Marshall 48
Mary II of England 45,62
Vera Massey 55
Henri Matisse vii,xvii
Clement Maydeston 40
Arthur Mekeel 55
Dr William Melton 42

Merganthaler 12
Horst Siegfried & Sylvia Meyer 48,56,66
David Miller xi
Peter Miller 66
Ted Milligan 55
David Miller viii,48
Tessa Mitchell 55
Deryck Moore 55
Annie Lavinia Morley 47
Frank Morley 47
Frank Leslie and George Eric Morley 47
Henry and Walter Morley viii,47
Valentine Morley 47
Bill Morrell x
Derek Mottram 56
Hugh Murray 55
James Nayler 55
Cathy Nelson vi
Éilis Nelson vi
Martin Nelson xviii,56, flaps
Muffin Nelson vi
Eilidh Newton viii,48
Sergei Nikitin 55
Patrick Nuttgens reverse flap
Mandy O'Sullivan viii,48
Graham Parry 66
Paulinus 1
John Perott 42
Elaine Phillips 55
Pablo Picasso vi,vii,ix,xvii
Camille Pisarro vii
David Potter vii,8,66
John Potts reverse flap
J. B. Priestley 62,66

Philip Quinlan	66
Graham Ralph	55
James Ray	30,45
Henri Riviere	vii
Suzanne Eades Roberts	55
Nicholas Rogers	ix,65
Ian Campbell Ross	vi
Thomas Rotherham	41
George Rouault	vi
Joseph Rowntree	66
David Rubinstein	vii,55,66
David Rymer	reverse flap
Thomas Sander	41,42
Stephen Sayers	viii,ix, reverse flap
Swea Sayers	viii
Arnold Scalway	56
Norman Scooter	66
Lesley Seeger	viii,x,xvii,xviii,49,56,66
Aloys Senefelder	vi,11, 31
Bill Sessions	ix,7,30,48,51,52,56,66
Edith M Sessions	viii
Ethylwyn Margaret (Margot) Sessions	51
E. Sue Sessions	viii,48
James Michael Sessions	reverse flap
Joanna Mary (Jo) Sessions	viii,48
Mary Sessions	51
Michael Sessions	viii,xviii,6,30,48, 55,56,62,63,65
Paddy Sessions	56
Sebastian Kenji Sessions	reverse flap
Timothy Jonathan Sessions	viii,48,56
William Sessions	51
W Mark Sessions	56
Mike Sibley	viii
Alfred Sisley	vii
John Smart	ix
Carole Smith	55
John Sotheran	vii,6,47
William Sotheran	viii,48
Amanda Sowden	66
David Sox	55
Sian Statters	viii,48
Jaques Sterne	5,30,66
Laurence Sterne	vi,5,30,45,62
Elizabeth Stoner	56
William Storry	47
William Francis Storry	47
Marjorie Sykes	55
Fox Talbot	12
Paul Thorpe	55
Christine Trevett	55
Ann Tuke	reverse flap
Vahe Nersissens, Koko's bar and cafe, Goodramgate, York	xi
Maurice de Vlaminck	viii
Keith Walls	viii,ix,xi,xvii,60,66
Thomas Wanless	5,29,45,66
Norman Waddleton	viii,27
Gerry & Judy Webb	66
William III the Duke of Orange	4,45,62
John Wheater	47
Grace White	5,62
John White	5,4,24,45,62
W.T. Wickeley	47
B. Wickeley	47
John Woodcock	xi,60
John Woolman	55
Kathy Worsley (Duchess of Kent)	viii,6,26